versatile
VEGETARIAN

Versatile VEGETARIAN

150 Easy Recipes for Every Day

MACMILLAN • USA

MACMILLAN
A Simon & Schuster Macmillan Company
1633 Broadway
New York, NY 10019
Text copyright © 1997 Weight Watchers, International, Inc.

a word about
WEIGHT WATCHERS

Since 1963, Weight Watchers has grown from a handful of people to millions of enrollees annually. Today, Weight Watchers is recognized as the leading name in safe and sensible weight control. Weight Watchers members form a diverse group, from youths to senior citizens, attending meetings virtually around the globe.

Weight-loss and weight-management results vary by individual, but we recommend that you attend Weight Watchers meetings, follow the Weight Watchers food plan and participate in regular physical activity. For the Weight Watchers meeting nearest you, call 1-800-651-6000.

Weight Watchers Publishing Group

Editorial Director: Nancy Gagliardi
Senior Editor: Martha Schueneman
Food and Nutrition Editor: Regina Ragone, M.S., R.D.
Editorial Assistant: Christine Senft, M.S.
Recipe Developers: Joyce Hendley, M.S. and
  Tamara Holt

Nutrition Consultant: Mindy Hermann,
  M.B.A., R.D.
Photographer: David Bishop
Food Stylist: Mariann Sauvion
Book Design: Rachael McBrearty

Library of Congress Cataloging-in-Publication Data
Weight Watchers versatile vegetarian : 150 easy recipes for every day.
p. cm.
Includes index.
ISBM 0-02-861852-1
1. Vegetarian cookery. I. Weight Watchers International.
RM236.W45 1997   97-4285
641.5'636--dc21   CIP

Manufactured in the United States of America
10 9 8 7 6 5 4 3

table of
CONTENTS

INTRODUCTION

If you're like a good majority of the nation, you're probably not quite ready to part with your beloved sirloin, but you are making a valiant effort to cut down on your meat eating and to include more chicken, fish and pasta in your family-dinner repertoire. In other words, you've probably become a part-time vegetarian without even realizing it.

Based on the USDA Food Guide Pyramid (the national guideline for healthy eating), you should strive for a diet that features meat as a side dish, rather than as the main course. Nutrition experts agree that the health reasons for easing up on all meat are compelling: Although it's an excellent source of protein and iron, some cuts of meat can have large amounts of fat, specifically the dreaded saturated fat that can contribute to a host of ills, including overweight.

This new, nutritional perspective means that nowadays vegetarian recipes aren't viewed as unusual or offbeat—and *Weight Watchers Versatile Vegetarian* proves it. *Versatile Vegetarian* provides 150 luscious recipes for vegetarian dishes that are surprisingly similar to your family's meat-based favorites. These dishes focus on familiar foods that are appealing to the eye and delicious to the taste buds. We've also kept lifestyle in mind, making sure that the recipes won't keep you in the kitchen and including meal suggestions, neat hints, sound advice and how-tos for ensuring your eating habits are healthier.

Dig into a generous portion of rich Creamy Spinach and Pepper Lasagna or Rigatoni with "Meat" Sauce—you may be surprised that it's not the real thing. You'll find kid-friendly fare like Black Bean Chili, Lentil Burgers (try them with the "fries" from page 115) and Macaroni and Cheese, as well as new twists on old standbys: Potato and Egg Salad sneaks a little more protein—and a lot less fat—into the picnic perennial; Chunky Guacamole is a tasty way to get more veggies into your diet, and savory Spicy Baked Sweet Potato Chips will be a hit at your next party. When you're pressed for time, turn to one-skillet meals like Vegetable Fried Rice or the Basque specialty Pipérade; if it's a wintry weekend, Mexican Casserole, Vegetable-Bean Gratin or Rice and Chickpea–Stuffed Cabbage would be warming, filling and delicious.

If you've been toying with the idea of going the full-time vegetarian route or if you're already a part-time veg, *Versatile Vegetarian* will supply you with helpful ideas for including more soy (deliciously) into your diet; how to eat like a vegetarian in a restaurant; ways to reap more protein from produce and grains; sober advice on why you should go meatless; how to wean your family from meat; and more.

Another bonus: *Versatile Vegetarian* includes simple symbols to provide an at-a-glance sign reference for a recipe's features. For example, if a dish can be made ahead, frozen or prepared in about 20 minutes (start to finish), these easy-to-read symbols tell you in a flash, without your having to read the recipe. They also notify you in an instant if a recipe is spicy—some of the Thai- and Indian-influenced dishes are—or microwavable.

Whatever your goal—to lose or maintain weight, eat healthier or ease your family into a more nutritious eating style—*Versatile Vegetarian* will put you well on your way.

chapter one

BASICS

Vegetable Broth

makes 6 cups (12 servings)

Vegetable Broth can be hard to find sometimes; keep this easy vegetable broth on hand because the store-bought variety can also be expensive. To freeze it, spray a 12-cup muffin tin with nonstick cooking spray; ladle ¼ cup broth into each cup and freeze. When the broth is solid, pop each out of the tin and freeze in resealable freezer bags.

hint

Check out the wide array of healthful, meatless convenience foods available in natural foods stores: bean chilis and soups, grain and pasta mixes, vegetarian baked beans or fat-free refried beans, flavored soy products like tamari and barbecued, marinated tempeh patties are just a few. There are also fat-free meatless cold cuts: bologna, roast turkey and country ham make delicious sandwiches.

make ahead

one pot

2 teaspoons vegetable oil

3 carrots, chopped

2 leeks, cleaned and sliced

2 celery stalks, including leaves, chopped

2 onions, chopped

¼ cup tomato paste (no salt added)

4 parsley sprigs

6 basil leaves

4 garlic cloves

8 peppercorns

1 bay leaf

1. In a large saucepan, heat the oil. Add the carrots, leeks, celery and onions; cook, stirring as needed, until softened, about 10 minutes. Stir in the tomato paste, parsley, basil and garlic; cook 1 minute.

2. Add the peppercorns, bay leaf and 7 cups water; bring to a boil. Reduce the heat and simmer, covered, about 1 hour. Strain, discarding the solids. Refrigerate, covered, up to 1 week, or freeze up to 3 months.

serving provides: 17 Bonus Calories.

per serving: 17 Calories, 0 g Total Fat, 0 g Saturated Fat, 0 mg Cholesterol, 41 mg Sodium, 4 g Total Carbohydrate, 0 g Dietary Fiber, 0 g Protein, 0 mg Calcium.

POINTS **per serving:** 0.

Tomato Sauce

makes 4 cups (8 servings)

Most commercial tomato sauces are loaded with sodium. Make a huge batch of this sauce when canned Italian tomatoes are on sale and freeze in 1- and 2-cup portions. If you want a chunky sauce, don't press the sauce through the sieve.

We've deliberately omitted the herbs and spices from this sauce to keep it versatile. As you use the sauce, stir in basil and oregano for Italian recipes, chili powder and cumin for a Mexican flavor, or even brown sugar and vinegar for a barbecue sauce.

2 teaspoons vegetable oil

2 onions, chopped

2 garlic cloves, minced

One 35-ounce can Italian tomatoes (no salt added), cut up

¼ teaspoon salt

1. In a large nonstick skillet, heat the oil. Add the onions; cook, stirring as needed, until softened, about 5 minutes. Add the garlic; cook, stirring, 1 minute. Stir in the tomatoes and salt; cook until thickened, about 15 minutes.

2. Transfer to a blender or food processor and puree. Transfer to a sieve and press through with a spatula. Refrigerate, covered, up to 1 week, or freeze up to 3 months.

serving provides: 1 Fruit/Vegetable.

per serving: 48 Calories, 1 g Total Fat, 0 g Saturated Fat, 0 mg Cholesterol, 90 mg Sodium, 8 g Total Carbohydrate, 3 g Dietary Fiber, 2 g Protein, 41 mg Calcium.

POINTS per serving: 0.

make ahead

one pot

rush hour

Yogurt Cheese

makes 1 ½ cups (4 servings)

When yogurt is drained to remove the whey, or liquid, it becomes a wonderfully thick, spreadable cheese. If you strain it for as little as 5 hours it will be slightly thickened (like sour cream), but if you have the time to strain it for 2 days, it will be quite firm (like cream cheese). Flavor it with herbs, spices, garlic or even chopped dried fruit and honey. Spread it on crackers, bagels, pancakes; use it instead of sour cream in your favorite dip—experiment! And don't discard the whey—use it, instead of water or milk, when making bread or biscuits.

3 cups plain nonfat yogurt

Spoon the yogurt into a coffee filter or cheesecloth-lined strainer; place over a bowl. Refrigerate, covered, at least 5 hours.

serving provides: 1 Protein/Milk.

per serving: 66 Calories, 0 g Total Fat, 0 g Saturated Fat, 2 mg Cholesterol, 72 mg Sodium, 7 g Total Carbohydrate, 0 g Dietary Fiber, 9 g Protein, 213 mg Calcium.

POINTS per serving: 1.

make ahead

Tofu Salad Dressing

makes 1 cup (8 servings)

This salad dressing is similar to mayonnaise. Flavor it with herbs, vinegar or lemon juice.

½ **pound silken tofu**

4 **teaspoons olive oil**

2 **tablespoons white-wine vinegar**

½ **garlic clove, crushed**

1 **teaspoon Dijon mustard**

½ **teaspoon salt**

In a blender or food processor, puree the tofu, oil, vinegar, garlic, mustard and salt. Refrigerate in an airtight container up to 1 week.

serving provides: 1 Fat.

per serving: 38 Calories, 3 g Total Fat, 0 g Saturated Fat, 0 mg Cholesterol, 167 mg Sodium, 1 g Total Carbohydrate, 0 g Dietary Fiber, 2 g Protein, 12 mg Calcium.

POINTS **per serving:** 1.

make ahead

Beans

There are two steps to cooking beans: soaking and cooking. Soaking allows dried beans to absorb water, which makes them start to dissolve the gaseous starches that can cause discomfort. Cooking beans makes them tender and digestible. And rinsing them after soaking and draining any water after cooking will further help to reduce the gas-producing starches. Soaking and cooking dried beans is neither difficult nor complicated. If you think preparing beans is a lot of work, try our simple suggestions.

Soaking Beans

NOTE: Lentils, split peas and black-eyed peas do not need to be soaked.

Pick through the beans, discarding any discolored or shriveled beans or any foreign matter. Rinse well.

- **Traditional Slow Soak:** In a 5-quart saucepan, cover 1 pound dried beans with 10 cups water. Cover tightly and refrigerate 6–8 hours or overnight. Drain and rinse the beans.

- **Hot Soak:** In a 5-quart saucepan, bring 10 cups water to a boil. Add 1 pound dried beans and return to a boil. Remove from the heat; cover tightly and set aside at room temperature 2–3 hours. Drain and rinse the beans.

- **Quick Soak:** In a 5-quart saucepan, bring 10 cups water to a boil. Add 1 pound dried beans and return to a boil; let boil 2–3 minutes. Cover tightly and set aside at room temperature 1 hour. Drain and rinse the beans.

- **Gas-Free Soak:** (The best method for gas-free beans, developed by the California Dry Bean Advisory Board.) In a 5-quart saucepan, place 1 pound of beans in 10 or more cups of boiling water; boil for 2–3 minutes, cover and set aside overnight. By morning, 75 to 90 percent of the indigestible sugars will have dissolved into the soaking water. Drain, then rinse the beans thoroughly before cooking them.

Cooking Beans

When cooking beans, do not add salt or acidic ingredients, like vinegar, tomatoes or juice—which slow the cooking substantially; add these ingredients when the beans are just tender. Cooking times vary with the types of beans used but also may vary with their age. Beans are done when they can be easily mashed between two fingers or with a fork. Always test a few beans in case they have not cooked evenly.

1. Return the soaked, rinsed beans to the 5-quart saucepan. Cover the beans with 3 times their volume of water. Add herbs or spices (not salt), as desired.

2. Bring to a boil; reduce the heat and simmer gently, uncovered, stirring occasionally, until tender (the time will depend on the type of bean, but start checking after 45–60

make ahead

minutes). Do not boil them since this will break the skins. Check the level of the water and add more if it gets low.

3. When the beans are tender, drain and use in recipes; or for later use, immerse them in cold water until cool, then drain well and freeze in 1- to 2-cup packages. One pound of dried beans will yield about 5 or 6 cups cooked beans.

Pressure Cooking

This is one of the quickest ways to cook beans.

After you've soaked ½ pound of beans, place them in a 4-quart pressure cooker with 4 cups water. Cook at 15 pounds pressure following the manufacturer's directions for the type of legume you are cooking.

Pressed Tofu

Pressing tofu gives it a firm texture and helps it to absorb flavors better.
This recipe can easily be halved or doubled.

**½ pound reduced-fat firm tofu,
halved lengthwise**

Place the tofu in a single layer between two flat plates. Weight the top with a heavy can or similar object; the sides of the tofu should be bulging slightly but not cracking. Let stand 30 minutes–1 hour, then pour off and discard the water that accumulates. Do not press the tofu for longer than 1 hour. Use immediately or refrigerate, covered, up to 2 days.

serving provides: 1 Protein/Milk.

per serving: 34 Calories, 2 g Total Fat, 0 g Saturated Fat, 0 mg Cholesterol, 20 mg Sodium, 1 g Total Carbohydrate, 0 g Dietary Fiber, 4 g Protein, 14 mg Calcium.

POINTS per serving: 1.

hint
Experiment with plain nonfat yogurt. Mix with herbs and try making creamy pasta sauces, dips and salad dressings.

make ahead

Frozen Tofu

makes 4 servings

Freezing gives tofu a meat-like, chewy texture that's perfect for casseroles and stews. Frozen tofu can be stored up to 3 months; it's so versatile that you'll always want to keep some on hand.

½ pound reduced-fat firm tofu, halved lengthwise

1. Place the tofu in a single layer on a plate and cover tightly with plastic wrap. Freeze until firm, at least 1 hour.

2. Thaw in the refrigerator until soft, 6–8 hours. Squeeze the tofu to eliminate excess water. Crumble or grate into small pieces to achieve the desired texture. (Don't make the pieces too big—they will be overly chewy.)

serving provides: 1 Protein/Milk.

per serving: 34 Calories, 2 g Total Fat, 0 g Saturated Fat, 0 mg Cholesterol, 20 mg Sodium, 1 g Total Carbohydrate, 0 g Dietary Fiber, 4 g Protein, 14 mg Calcium.

POINTS **per serving:** 1.

hint

To grill tofu, cut firm, reduced-fat tofu into 2x1x½" cubes. Marinate in reduced-sodium soy sauce, grated gingerroot, garlic and rice wine or sherry for about 4 hours, turning occasionally. Thread on metal skewers and grill until lightly browned, about 5–8 minutes.

make ahead

Mustard-Vinaigrette Dressing

makes 8 servings

This delicious classic makes store-bought versions pale by comparison, with quite a bit less fat. It will keep in the refrigerator up to 1 week.

hint

Try making a Szechuan salad dressing by combining soy sauce, rice vinegar, a bit of honey and hot chili pepper oil.

¼ cup Vegetable Broth (page 2)

3 tablespoons extra virgin olive oil

4 teaspoons red-wine vinegar

1 teaspoon Dijon mustard

½ garlic clove, minced

1 tablespoon minced fresh herbs (tarragon, basil or thyme), or 1 teaspoon dried

Pinch salt

Freshly ground black pepper, to taste

In a small jar with a tight-fitting lid or in a small bowl, combine the broth, oil, vinegar, mustard, garlic, herbs, salt and pepper; cover and shake well, or whisk until smooth. Pour into a serving container; refrigerate, covered, until needed. Shake well before using.

serving provides: 1 Fat.

per serving: 47 Calories, 5 g Total Fat, 1 g Saturated Fat, 0 mg Cholesterol, 24 mg Sodium, 1 g Total Carbohydrate, 0 g Dietary Fiber, 0 g Protein, 2 mg Calcium.

POINTS per serving: 1.

make ahead

one pot

Peanut Sauce

makes 6 servings

Craving the taste of peanuts but not all the fat? This nutty, spicy Thai condiment is traditionally served as a dipping sauce with the grilled vegetable skewers called satays. It's also wonderful tossed with cold pasta noodles; or spread it on wedges of pita bread for a filling snack. It will keep in the refrigerator up to 1 week; just thin it with water to the consistency you prefer.

1 cup rinsed drained canned chickpeas

¼ cup Vegetable Broth (page 2)

¼ cup creamy natural peanut butter

1 tablespoon soy sauce

1 garlic clove, minced

¼–½ teaspoon hot chile paste★

1 tablespoon minced cilantro (optional)

In a food processor or blender, puree the chickpeas, broth, peanut butter, soy sauce, garlic and chile paste. Thin with a few tablespoons water, if necessary, to the desired consistency. Refrigerate in an airtight container up to 1 week. Sprinkle with the cilantro (if using) just before serving.

serving provides: 1 Protein/Milk, 1 Fat.

per serving: 146 Calories, 8 g Total Fat, 2 g Saturated Fat, 0 mg Cholesterol, 314 mg Sodium, 13 g Total Carbohydrate, 4 g Dietary Fiber, 6 g Protein, 21 mg Calcium.

POINTS per serving: 3.

hint
Peanut butter is a great source of nonmeat protein, but watch the fat. Some brands contain as much as 9 grams of fat per tablespoon. But reduced-fat peanut butter is not the answer because the fat has been replaced with sugar.

★ Made from mashed red hot chile peppers, vinegar and seasonings (often including garlic), hot chile paste is a pungent condiment that adds fiery zest to many dishes. Stored in the refrigerator, it will keep well over a year, but its potency will decrease as it ages. Find it in Asian markets and gourmet grocery stores; if unavailable, substitute crushed red pepper flakes.

make ahead

spicy

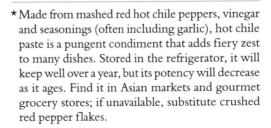

Perfect Brown Rice

For nutrient and fiber content—not to mention flavor—chewy, nutty brown rice beats white rice anytime. Although it takes a little longer to cook, this easy procedure makes it well worth it. Cooked rice freezes beautifully, so make a double batch and store it in freezer bags; thaw it in a bowl of hot water or in the microwave (open the bag first). Resist the temptation to lift the lid as the rice cooks since heat will be lost when the steam escapes.

1 cup brown rice

Pinch salt

Bring 2¼ cups water to a boil. Add the rice slowly, so that the boiling doesn't stop; stir in the salt. Reduce the heat and simmer, covered (without lifting the cover), until tender, 35–40 minutes. Fluff with a fork just before serving.

serving provides: 1 Bread.

per serving: 114 Calories, 1 g Total Fat, 0 g Saturated Fat, 0 mg Cholesterol, 27 mg Sodium, 24 g Total Carbohydrate, 1 g Dietary Fiber, 2 g Protein, 7 mg Calcium.

POINTS **per serving:** 2.

make ahead

one pot

chapter two

SOUPS &
APPETIZERS

Chickpea Soup

makes 4 servings

This soup is rich and creamy but contains no cream: The pureed chickpeas provide the velvety smooth texture.

1 teaspoon vegetable oil

1 onion, chopped

3 garlic cloves, minced

One 19-ounce can chickpeas, rinsed and drained

1½ teaspoons minced fresh sage, or ½ teaspoon dried

¼ teaspoon freshly ground black pepper

2 cups Vegetable Broth (page 2)

Half 10-ounce package frozen chopped spinach, thawed and squeezed dry

½ teaspoon salt

2 tablespoons fresh lemon juice

1. In a medium saucepan, heat the oil. Add the onion; cook, stirring as needed, until softened, about 5 minutes. Add the garlic; cook, stirring, 1 minute. Stir in the chickpeas, sage and pepper.

2. Stir in the broth, spinach and salt; bring to a boil. Transfer the mixture to a blender or food processor; puree. Return to the saucepan and simmer 5 minutes; stir in the lemon juice.

serving provides: 2 Protein/Milks.

per serving: 163 Calories, 3 g Total Fat, 0 g Saturated Fat, 0 mg Cholesterol, 590 mg Sodium, 25 g Total Carbohydrate, 7 g Dietary Fiber, 9 g Protein, 99 mg Calcium.

POINTS per serving: 2.

make ahead

one pot

rush hour

Cabbage and Bean Soup

makes 4 servings

If you prefer, substitute water or a combination of broth and water for the vegetable broth.

1 tablespoon + 1 teaspoon olive oil

2 celery stalks, thinly sliced

1½ onions, thinly sliced

3 garlic cloves, minced

3 cups Vegetable Broth (page 2)

2 cups coarsely chopped green cabbage

One 15-ounce can pinto, navy or great Northern beans, rinsed and drained

One 14-ounce can diced plum tomatoes (no salt added)

½ teaspoon dried thyme

½ teaspoon salt

¼ cup grated Parmesan cheese

Freshly ground black pepper, to taste

1. In a medium saucepan, heat the oil. Add the celery, onions and garlic; cook, stirring as needed, until softened, about 5 minutes.

2. Stir in the broth, cabbage, beans, tomatoes, thyme and salt; bring to a boil. Reduce the heat and simmer, stirring as needed, 45 minutes. Serve, sprinkled with the cheese and pepper.

serving provides: 1 Fruit/Vegetable, 2 Protein/Milks, 1 Fat.

per serving: 209 Calories, 7 g Total Fat, 2 g Saturated Fat, 4 mg Cholesterol, 696 mg Sodium, 30 g Total Carbohydrate, 7 g Dietary Fiber, 9 g Protein, 169 mg Calcium.

POINTS **per serving:** 3.

hint
Refrigerate soups overnight. Skim off the fat that hardens on top before reheating.

make ahead

one pot

Sweet Pea Soup

makes 4 servings

This is a delicate soup, perfect for a light summer lunch. The shot of lime juice really heightens the flavors.

2 teaspoons olive oil

1 onion, chopped

One 20-ounce bag frozen peas, thawed

¼ cup chopped mint

½ teaspoon salt

¼ teaspoon freshly ground black pepper

¼ cup fresh lime juice

1. In a medium saucepan, heat the oil. Add the onion; cook, stirring as needed, until softened, about 5 minutes. Add the peas; cook, stirring as needed, until tender, 6–7 minutes.

2. Transfer the mixture to a blender or food processor. Add the mint, salt, and 2 cups water; puree. Refrigerate, covered, until chilled, at least 2 hours. Stir in the lime juice.

serving provides: 2 Breads, 1 Fat.

per serving: 163 Calories, 3 g Total Fat, 0 g Saturated Fat, 0 mg Cholesterol, 433 mg Sodium, 27 g Total Carbohydrate, 10 g Dietary Fiber, 9 g Protein, 53 mg Calcium.

POINTS per serving: 2.

make ahead

one pot

Tofu Miso Soup

makes 4 servings

Miso is a fermented soybean paste used to thicken and season Japanese dishes. It ranges in color from dark brown to beige; shiro miso is the lightest in both color and flavor. Miso is available in Asian markets as well as most natural foods stores. Refrigerated, in an airtight container, it will keep for several months.

3 tablespoons light (shiro) miso

4 cups Vegetable Broth (page 2)

1 pound silken tofu, cubed

2 scallions, thinly sliced

1. In a small bowl, dissolve the miso in 1 cup of the broth.

2. In a medium saucepan, bring the remaining 3 cups broth to a boil. Stir in the miso, tofu and scallions; cook until heated through, about 5 minutes.

serving provides: 2 Protein/Milks.

per serving: 130 Calories, 4 g Total Fat, 1 g Saturated Fat, 0 mg Cholesterol, 593 mg Sodium, 14 g Total Carbohydrate, 1 g Dietary Fiber, 11 g Protein, 47 mg Calcium.

POINTS **per serving:** 3.

hint
Although bland on its own, tofu, or soybean curd, takes on the flavors of whatever foods or spices it is combined with. Tofu comes in firm (chop into stir-fried dishes or press out moisture, marinate and grill), soft (dice into soups) and silken (puree into sauces, shakes and desserts).

one pot

rush hour

Indian Tomato-Lentil Soup

makes 4 servings

To transform this fragrant soup into a full meal, add some Perfect Brown Rice (page 12) when you return the pureed lentils to the mixture.

(page 12)

1 tablespoon olive oil

1 onion, chopped

2 tablespoons grated peeled ginger-root

4 garlic cloves, minced

1 teaspoon ground cumin

½ teaspoon ground coriander

One 14-ounce can crushed tomatoes (no salt added)

1 cup dried lentils, picked over, rinsed and drained

½ teaspoon salt

2 teaspoons fresh lemon juice

¼ cup chopped cilantro

1. In a medium saucepan, heat the oil. Add the onion; cook, stirring as needed, until softened, about 5 minutes. Add the ginger, garlic, cumin and coriander; cook, stirring, 1 minute.

2. Stir in the tomatoes, lentils, salt and 4 cups water; bring to a boil. Reduce the heat and simmer until the lentils are soft, 35–45 minutes. Transfer 2 cups of the lentil mixture to a blender or food processor and puree. Return the mixture to the saucepan and simmer until heated through, about 5 minutes. Serve, drizzled with the lemon juice and sprinkled with the cilantro.

serving provides: 1 Fruit/Vegetable, 2 Protein/Milks, 1 Fat.

per serving: 236 Calories, 4 g Total Fat, 1 g Saturated Fat, 0 mg Cholesterol, 314 mg Sodium, 37 g Total Carbohydrate, 17 g Dietary Fiber, 15 g Protein, 75 mg Calcium.

POINTS per serving: 2.

(See photo insert.)

---

hint

Be liberal with sprouts: Bean sprouts (the thick, white strands) have a bittersweet crunch, perfect for stir-fried dishes; and the nutty taste of alfalfa sprouts (the thin strands with tiny nuts) are perfect for stuffing into sandwiches or sprinkling over soups and salads.

make ahead

one pot

spicy

Vegetable-Noodle Soup

makes 4 servings

This soup is so chock-full of veggies that's it's almost a stew—perfect for lunch on a wintry day after a morning of sledding.

2 teaspoons olive oil

1 fennel bulb, diced

2 carrots, diced

1 onion, chopped

3 garlic cloves, minced

4 cups Vegetable Broth (page 2)

2 cups coarsely chopped Swiss chard leaves

¾ cup elbow macaroni

¼ teaspoon salt

¼ cup chopped flat-leaf parsley

¼ teaspoon freshly ground black pepper

1. In a medium saucepan, heat the oil. Add the fennel, carrots, onion and garlic; cook, stirring as needed, until the fennel and onion are golden, 10–12 minutes.

2. Stir in the broth, chard, macaroni and salt; cook until the macaroni is tender, about 10 minutes. Stir in the parsley and pepper.

serving provides: 1 Bread, 2 Fruit/Vegetables, 1 Fat.

per serving: 170 Calories, 3 g Total Fat, 0 g Saturated Fat, 0 mg Cholesterol, 300 mg Sodium, 32 g Total Carbohydrate, 3 g Dietary Fiber, 5 g Protein, 51 mg Calcium.

POINTS per serving: 3.

make ahead

one pot

rush hour

Potato-Watercress Soup

makes 4 servings

*Although we think this soup deliciously refreshing on a hot summer day,
it's equally good warm. If you find watercress too peppery, substitute chopped
spinach leaves.*

2 teaspoons olive oil

1½ onions, chopped

**4 large all-purpose potatoes, peeled
and diced**

1½ cups Vegetable Broth (page 2)

2 garlic cloves, minced

1 cup trimmed watercress

1 cup low-fat (1%) milk

½ teaspoon salt

**¼ teaspoon freshly ground black
pepper**

1. In a large saucepan, heat the oil. Add the onions; cook, stirring as needed, until softened, about 5 minutes. Add the potatoes, broth and garlic; bring to a boil. Reduce the heat and simmer until the potatoes are tender, about 20 minutes. Stir in the watercress.

2. Transfer the mixture to a blender or food processor; add the milk and puree. Stir in the salt and pepper. Return the mixture to the saucepan and simmer 5 minutes. Refrigerate, covered, until chilled, about 2 hours. Thin with additional broth or water, if necessary, to the desired consistency.

serving provides: 2 Breads, 1 Fruit/Vegetable, 1 Fat.

per serving: 254 Calories, 3 g Total Fat, 1 g Saturated Fat, 2 mg Cholesterol, 368 mg Sodium, 51 g Total Carbohydrate, 5 g Dietary Fiber, 7 g Protein, 115 mg Calcium.

POINTS **per serving:** 4.

make ahead

Good Advice

If you're ready to go vegetarian, you won't be alone: *Vegetarian Times* magazine estimates that there are at least 12 million vegetarians in the United States, with anywhere from 1 to 7 percent of them considered to be "true" or lacto-ovo vegetarians, meaning they eat a plant-based diet that also includes milk and eggs. A larger percentage of the population is considered "semi-vegetarian"—they occasionally eat fish or chicken. "Casual vegetarians" eat vegetarian meals five days a week, reverting to meat on the weekends. Vegans (pronounced vee-ghuns) eat an entirely plant-based diet that excludes milk, eggs and usually honey.

A low-fat vegetarian diet offers the best prevention against heart disease, but you won't automatically lose weight since you still must watch your calorie intake.

For years, many had thought that vegetarians needed to eat certain foods at the same meals, such as rice and beans, in order to get complete proteins. But modern nutrition science has exposed this as a myth. Also, you won't get anemia from giving up meat. Although beef is an excellent source of iron, plant foods and cereals have iron, too. As long as you're eating a variety of nutritious foods—especially those high in iron and vitamin C—you don't need to worry.

Butternut Squash Soup

makes 4 servings

The velvety texture of pureed squash and the fresh flavor of orange make this soup an elegant beginning to an autumn meal.

One 2-pound butternut squash, peeled, seeded and cut into 1" chunks

1½ cups Vegetable Broth (page 2)

1 cup orange juice

½ teaspoon salt

¼ cup chopped basil

¼ teaspoon freshly ground black pepper

1. In a medium saucepan, bring the squash and broth to a boil. Reduce the heat and simmer until tender, 10–15 minutes.

2. Transfer the mixture to a blender or food processor. Add the orange juice and salt; puree. Return the mixture to the saucepan and simmer 5 minutes. Serve, sprinkled with the basil and pepper.

serving provides: 1 Bread, 1 Fruit/Vegetable.

per serving: 110 Calories, 0 g Total Fat, 0 g Saturated Fat, 0 mg Cholesterol, 328 mg Sodium, 28 g Total Carbohydrate, 3 g Dietary Fiber, 2 g Protein, 80 mg Calcium.

POINTS per serving: 2.

make ahead

one pot

rush hour

Spicy Black Bean Soup

makes 4 servings

To make this soup even spicier, serve it with hot red pepper sauce and chopped raw red onion. Make a double batch and freeze some for another meal—but don't add the cilantro, jalapeño and lemon juice until just before reheating.

1 cup dried black beans, picked over, rinsed and drained

2 teaspoons olive oil

1 green or red bell pepper, seeded and chopped

1 onion, chopped

2 garlic cloves, minced

½ teaspoon ground cumin

½ teaspoon crushed red pepper flakes

¼ teaspoon cinnamon

3 cups Vegetable Broth (page 2)

¼ cup tomato paste (no salt added)

1–2 jalapeño peppers, seeded, deveined and minced (wear gloves to prevent irritation)

2 tablespoons chopped cilantro

1 tablespoon fresh lemon juice

1. Soak the beans (see page 6).

2. In a large saucepan, heat the oil. Add the bell pepper, onion and garlic; cook, stirring as needed, until softened, about 5 minutes. Add the cumin, pepper flakes and cinnamon; cook, stirring, 30 seconds.

3. Stir in the beans and broth; bring to a boil. Stir in the tomato paste. Reduce the heat and simmer, covered, until the beans are very soft, 1½–2 hours.

4. Transfer half of the mixture to a blender or food processor and puree. Return the mixture half to the saucepan and simmer 5 minutes. Stir in the jalapeños, cilantro and lemon juice.

serving provides: 1 Fruit/Vegetable, 2 Protein/Milks, 1 Fat.

per serving: 251 Calories, 3 g Total Fat, 1 g Saturated Fat, 0 mg Cholesterol, 104 mg Sodium, 45 g Total Carbohydrate, 10 g Dietary Fiber, 13 g Protein, 91 mg Calcium.

POINTS **per serving:** 3.

hint
Soup and a sandwich is a nutritional, satisfying lunch. Boost a sandwich's nutrient tally by sliding in slices of raw zucchini, tomato, cucumber and sprouts.

make ahead

one pot

spicy

Split Pea Soup with Garlic Croutons

makes 4 servings

Rosemary gives this soup a pleasant flavor that complements the croutons.
The soup freezes well, so make a large batch in the beginning of winter and
enjoy it throughout the season.

4 cups Vegetable Broth (page 2)

3 carrots, diced

1 cup green split peas, picked over, rinsed and drained

2 onions, diced

1 garlic clove, minced

1 teaspoon minced rosemary

½ teaspoon salt

1 tablespoon olive oil

1 garlic clove, crushed

2 ounces French bread, cut into 12 rounds

¼ cup chopped flat-leaf parsley

1. In a large saucepan, combine the broth, carrots, peas, onions, minced garlic, rosemary and salt; bring to a boil. Reduce the heat and simmer, partially covered, stirring as needed, until the peas have disintegrated, 1–1¼ hours.

2. Preheat the oven to 350° F. In a small bowl, combine the oil and crushed garlic. Brush one side of the bread rounds with the garlic oil; place on a baking sheet. Bake until crisp, about 10 minutes.

3. Divide the soup among 4 bowls; on each, arrange 3 bread rounds on top and sprinkle with the parsley.

serving provides: 1 Bread, 1 Fruit/Vegetable, 2 Protein/Milks, 1 Fat.

per serving: 322 Calories, 5 g Total Fat, 1 g Saturated Fat, 0 mg Cholesterol, 490 mg Sodium, 56 g Total Carbohydrate, 16 g Dietary Fiber, 16 g Protein, 75 mg Calcium.

POINTS per serving: 4.

make ahead

one pot

Spicy Chickpea Samosas

makes 8 servings

These delicious bite-size turnovers are a popular Indian snack. They're usually made with potatoes, but chickpeas add a healthful protein boost. Traditionally, samosas are deep-fried; here baking makes them every bit as delicious without adding calories.

Dough

1½ cups all-purpose flour

1 teaspoon baking powder

¼ teaspoon salt

⅓ cup part-skim ricotta cheese

3 tablespoons low-fat (1%) milk

1 egg white

2 tablespoons vegetable oil

Filling

2 teaspoons vegetable oil

1 teaspoon curry powder

¼ teaspoon ground cumin

½ onion, finely chopped

One 1" piece gingerroot, peeled and minced

1 garlic clove, minced

One 15-ounce can chickpeas, rinsed and drained

1 tablespoon chopped green chiles

½ cup thawed frozen peas

1 tablespoon fresh lemon juice

¼ teaspoon salt

1. To prepare the dough, in a food processor, combine the flour, baking powder and salt; pulse to blend. Add the cheese, milk, egg white and oil; pulse until the dough begins to hold together. Gather into a ball, wrap in plastic and refrigerate at least 1 hour. (The dough may be wrapped in plastic and refrigerated up to 2 days at this point; let stand 1 hour at room temperature and proceed with recipe.)

2. To prepare the filling, in a large nonstick skillet, heat the oil. Add the curry and cumin; cook, stirring constantly, until just fragrant, about 30 seconds. Add the onion, ginger and garlic; cook, stirring as needed, until the onion is softened, about 5 minutes. Add the chickpeas, chiles and ¾ cup water; cook, stirring gently, until most of the liquid is evaporated, 4–5 minutes. Remove from the heat and mash until fairly smooth. Gently stir in the peas, lemon juice and salt, taking care not to mash the peas. Let stand 30 minutes.

3. Preheat the oven to 425° F. Spray a baking sheet with nonstick cooking spray. Sprinkle a work surface with a little flour. Place a small bowl of warm water by the work surface.

4. Divide the dough into fourths and roll each between your palms into a ball. Roll each ball into an 8" round and cut each in half. Moisten the straight edge of a dough half with a few drops of water. Fold over the straight edges, forming a cone, and press firmly to seal. Place about 2 tablespoons of the filling in the cone, then moisten the cone's open edges with a little water; firmly pinch the edges together. Repeat to make 8 samosas. Place the samosas on the baking sheet and spray them lightly on both sides with nonstick cooking spray. Bake 15 minutes, until lightly browned.

serving provides: 1 Bread, 1 Protein/Milk, 1 Fat.

per serving: 192 Calories, 6 g Total Fat, 1 g Saturated Fat, 3 mg Cholesterol, 286 mg Sodium, 26 g Total Carbohydrate, 3 g Dietary Fiber, 7 g Protein, 81 mg Calcium.

POINTS per serving: 4.

(See photo insert.)

make ahead

Good Advice

Most of us were raised with the notion that in order to grow strong and healthy, we needed to consume plenty of high-protein meat, chicken, fish and eggs. Today, we know that a diet high in animal protein isn't the best way to good health, especially since these proteins tend to be high in saturated fat.

If you've been toying with the idea of going vegetarian but are wary that you won't get enough protein, consider this: The average American consumes twice the recommended amount of protein. The Recommended Daily Allowance for protein is .8 grams of protein per kilogram of body weight—about 55 grams for a 150-pound person.

Tomato-Basil Bruschetta

makes 8 servings

Bruschetta (pronounced broo-SKET-ta) is simply Italian for "toasted bread," usually made with garlic. But oh, what a difference an Italian translation can make! For the prettiest hors d'oeuvres, use the long, slim French bread known as ficelle (pronounced fee-CELL; available in gourmet grocery stores and bakeries).

2 very ripe tomatoes, seeded and finely diced

1 tablespoon slivered basil (optional: reserve 2-3 sprigs for garnish)

1 tablespoon balsamic vinegar

2 teaspoons extra virgin olive oil

Pinch salt

Freshly ground black pepper, to taste

One 8-ounce loaf French or Italian bread, cut into 8 slices

1 garlic clove, halved

1. In a small bowl, combine the tomatoes, basil, vinegar, oil, salt and pepper. Set aside.

2. Preheat the oven to 375° F. Place the bread on a baking sheet in a single layer; toast until lightly browned, 2–3 minutes on each side.

3. Rub the toast slices on one side with the garlic clove and top with a generous tablespoon of the tomato mixture. Arrange on a serving tray and garnish with the basil leaves (if using). Let stand, covered, at room temperature until the mixture's juices have soaked into the bread, at least 30 minutes (but no longer than 6 hours before serving).

serving provides: 1 Bread.

per serving: 96 Calories, 2 g Total Fat, 0 g Saturated Fat, 0 mg Cholesterol, 194 mg Sodium, 17 g Total Carbohydrate, 1 g Dietary Fiber, 3 g Protein, 24 mg Calcium.

POINTS per serving: 2.

make ahead

Stuffed Endive Bites

makes 8 servings

Smoky Southwestern flavors are a perfect match for cool, elegant endive. Chipotles en adobo, smoked dried jalapeño peppers in a complex sauce of tomato, garlic and spices, can be found in the Mexican section of some supermarkets and in Latino grocery stores. Buy a small can and puree the contents; refrigerated, it will keep up to six months. Just a spoonful will add a smoky dazzle to soups, stews and other dishes.

hint
The ideal beverage for any meal? Water, plain and simple: It won't compete with a food's flavor, it fills you up and has zero calories. If you want something fizzy, have fruit-flavored, no-calorie seltzer.

4 Belgian endives

1 red bell pepper, roasted,★ and finely chopped

2 ounces nonfat cream cheese

1 tablespoon minced sweet onion

1–2 teaspoons pureed *chipotles en adobo*

Arugula leaves or watercress (optional)

1. Trim the bottoms of each endive and pull apart the leaves; set them aside. Mince the smallest leaves at the core.

2. In a medium bowl, combine the pepper, cream cheese, onion, minced endive and the *chipotles*. Dab a scant teaspoon of the pepper mixture onto the bottom of each endive leaf.

3. Line a serving tray with the arugula or watercress (if using); arrange the filled endive leaves on top in an overlapping starburst pattern. Serve at once, or refrigerate, covered, up to 6 hours.

serving provides: 1 Fruit/Vegetable.

per serving: 22 Calories, 0 g Total Fat, 0 g Saturated Fat, 0 mg Cholesterol, 76 mg Sodium, 4 g Total Carbohydrate, 2 g Dietary Fiber, 2 g Protein, 22 mg Calcium.

POINTS **per serving:** 0.

make ahead

rush hour

★ To roast bell pepper, preheat broiler. Line baking sheet with foil; place pepper on baking sheet. Broil 4–6" from heat, turning frequently with tongs, until skin is lightly charred on all sides. Transfer to paper bag; fold bag closed and let steam 10 minutes. Peel, seed and devein pepper over sink to drain juices.

"Stuffed" Cherry Tomatoes

makes 8 servings

Even though it's a breeze to make, this classy hors d'oeuvre never fails to impress—people will think you've spent hours in the kitchen. Experiment with the blue cheese component: Bleu de Bresse or Saga Blue work nicely. The recipe can be halved if your party's small. If your tomatoes have stems, trim a paper-thin slice off the bottom so they stand upright.

Two 1-pint baskets cherry tomatoes

¾ cup crumbled blue cheese

3 ounces nonfat cream cheese

2 teaspoons minced fresh thyme, or 1 teaspoon dried

Fresh thyme sprigs (optional)

1. Slice ¼" off the bottom of each tomato, reserving the bottoms.

2. In a small bowl, combine the cheeses and thyme. Dab about ½ teaspoon of the mixture on the cut edge of each tomato. Cover each with a tomato bottom. Arrange the tomatoes upside-down (the "dimples" on the stem end will keep them upright) on a large serving tray and garnish with the thyme sprigs (if using). Serve at once, or refrigerate, covered, up to 2 hours (let stand at room temperature 30 minutes before serving).

serving provides: 1 Fruit/Vegetable.

per serving: 72 Calories, 4 g Total Fat, 2 g Saturated Fat, 10 mg Cholesterol, 259 mg Sodium, 5 g Total Carbohydrate, 1 g Dietary Fiber, 5 g Protein, 82 mg Calcium.

POINTS per serving: 2.

make ahead

(See photo insert.)

Spicy Baked Sweet Potato Chips

makes 6 servings

These addictively delicious, chewy chips provide a nutritious dose of carotenoids—vegetable pigments believed to have health-promoting properties. To make sure your chips are cut thinly and evenly, use a vegetable slicer.

hint
Be wary of packaged vegetable chips. They're deep-fried and salted like potato chips and priced like semi-precious stones. Consider making your own low-fat versions by using this recipe as a starting point.

spicy

3 large sweet potatoes (1½ pounds), peeled and very thinly sliced

2 tablespoons vegetable oil

½ teaspoon curry powder

½ teaspoon paprika

¼ teaspoon salt

1. Pat the potato slices between paper towels to dry, then arrange in a single layer on several sheets of paper towel. Let stand 10 minutes, then place slices in a medium bowl. Preheat the oven to 375° F. Line two baking sheets with foil and spray with nonstick cooking spray.

2. In a small nonstick skillet, heat the oil. Add the curry powder; cook, stirring, until just fragrant, 15–20 seconds. Remove from the heat; stir in the paprika and drizzle over the potatoes. Sprinkle with the salt; toss to coat.

3. Arrange the potatoes in a single layer on the baking sheets and spray evenly with nonstick cooking spray. Bake until lightly browned, 12–15 minutes; turn and bake until slightly browned at the edges, 5–10 minutes longer (watch for burning). Place in a paper towel–lined serving bowl and serve warm.

serving provides: 1 Bread, 1 Fat.

per serving: 196 Calories, 5 g Total Fat, 1 g Saturated Fat, 0 mg Cholesterol, 112 mg Sodium, 37 g Total Carbohydrate, 5 g Dietary Fiber, 3 g Protein, 43 mg Calcium.
POINTS per serving: 3.

(See photo insert.)

Barley "Risotto" with Mushrooms

makes 4 servings

Barley makes an easy—and inexpensive—substitute for Arborio rice in this very rich dish. Its earthy flavor pairs beautifully with portobello mushrooms.

3 cups Vegetable Broth (page 2)

2 teaspoons olive oil

2 onions, finely chopped

2 portobello mushrooms, diced

2 garlic cloves, minced

½ cup pearl barley

1 tablespoon grated Parmesan cheese

¼ teaspoon minced thyme

1. In a medium saucepan, bring the broth to a boil. Reduce the heat and simmer.

2. In a large nonstick saucepan, heat the oil. Add the onions; cook, stirring as needed, until softened, about 5 minutes. Add the mushrooms and garlic; cook, stirring as needed, until the mushrooms are wilted, about 10 minutes. Add the barley; cook, stirring to coat, about 1 minute.

3. Stir in 1 cup of the broth; reduce the heat and simmer, covered, 5 minutes. Stir in another ½ cup of the broth; simmer, covered, 10 minutes longer. Continue adding broth, ½ cup at a time, stirring, while the broth is absorbed, until the barley is just tender. The total cooking time should be about 40–45 minutes. Stir in the cheese and thyme; serve at once.

serving provides: 1 Bread, 1 Fruit/Vegetable, 1 Fat.

per serving: 178 Calories, 3 g Total Fat, 1 g Saturated Fat, 1 mg Cholesterol, 92 mg Sodium, 32 g Total Carbohydrate, 5 g Dietary Fiber, 6 g Protein, 43 mg Calcium.

POINTS per serving: 3.

Roasted Caponata

makes 4 servings

Serve this delectable spread with a hearty peasant bread, or toss it with pasta.

1 small (¾-pound) eggplant, cubed

¾ teaspoon salt

2 celery stalks, diced

1 green bell pepper, seeded and diced

1 onion, diced

4 teaspoons olive oil

1 tomato, diced

2 garlic cloves, minced

6 large kalamata olives, pitted and minced

2 teaspoons red-wine vinegar

½ teaspoon freshly ground black pepper

1. Preheat the oven to 400° F. Place the eggplant on paper towels and sprinkle with ¼ teaspoon of the salt. Cover with a plate and press 20 minutes. Rinse and squeeze dry between more paper towels.

2. In a 13x9" baking dish, combine the eggplant, celery, bell pepper and onion; drizzle with the oil and toss to coat. Roast until golden, 20–30 minutes. Add the tomato and garlic; roast 20 minutes longer. Add the olives, vinegar, pepper and remaining ½ teaspoon salt. Cool to room temperature.

serving provides: 1 Fruit/Vegetable, 1 Fat.

per serving: 89 Calories, 6 g Total Fat, 1 g Saturated Fat, 0 mg Cholesterol, 372 mg Sodium, 10 g Total Carbohydrate, 3 g Dietary Fiber, 2 g Protein, 33 mg Calcium.

POINTS **per serving:** 2.

hint
If you think your family won't eat whole-wheat pasta, try mixing a batch of half regular with half whole-wheat, then top with rich tomato sauce.

make ahead

one pot

Tzaziki

makes 4 servings

Tzaziki, a traditional dip-like Greek appetizer, is delicious with pita triangles or fresh vegetables. For a thicker consistency, make it with Yogurt Cheese instead of yogurt. If you can find English (sometimes called hothouse) cucumbers, use only one; they're seedless, so you can eliminate that step, and you don't need to peel them, either.

3 cucumbers, peeled, seeded, grated and squeezed dry

1 cup plain nonfat yogurt or Yogurt Cheese (page 4)

2 teaspoons chopped mint

2 teaspoons extra virgin olive oil

1–2 garlic cloves, crushed

¼ teaspoon salt

¼ teaspoon freshly ground black pepper

In a small bowl, combine the cucumbers, yogurt, mint, oil and garlic. Stir in the salt and pepper. Refrigerate, covered, until chilled, about 2 hours.

serving provides: 1 Fruit/Vegetable, 1 Fat.

per serving: 67 Calories, 2 g Total Fat, 0 g Saturated Fat, 1 mg Cholesterol, 191 mg Sodium, 8 g Total Carbohydrate, 1 g Dietary Fiber, 4 g Protein, 131 mg Calcium.

POINTS per serving: 1.

hint
Make cucumber "daisies" by peeling a cucumber and running a fork along the length of it, making grooves with the tines from one end of the cucumber to the other. Rotate the cucumber and repeat until it is covered with grooves. Slice the cucumber crosswise and you'll get ruffled edges on every slice.

make ahead

Sweet and Spicy Indian Dumplings

These dumplings are similar to a specialty of southern India, where they are a common snack. Serve them with your favorite spicy Indian chutney.

½ **cup cooked green peas**

½ **cup plain nonfat yogurt**

¼ **cup shredded coconut**

¼ **cup unsalted dry-roasted cashews, chopped**

¼ **cup chopped cilantro**

1 **tablespoon grated peeled gingerroot**

½ **teaspoon salt**

1 **cup instant farina**

¾ **cup boiling water**

Pinch baking soda

1 **tablespoon vegetable oil**

1. In a medium bowl, combine the peas, yogurt, coconut, cashews, cilantro, ginger and salt. In a small bowl, combine the farina and water; add to the yogurt mixture. Stir in the baking soda. Divide the mixture into 16 balls and flatten them gently.

2. In a large nonstick skillet, heat the oil. Add the balls and cook until golden, 5 minutes on each side.

serving provides: 2 Breads, 1 Fat.

per serving: 173 Calories, 10 g Total Fat, 3 g Saturated Fat, 1 mg Cholesterol, 368 mg Sodium, 17 g Total Carbohydrate, 2 g Dietary Fiber, 5 g Protein, 85 mg Calcium.

POINTS per serving: 4.

rush hour

spicy

White Bean–Pesto Dip

makes 4 servings

This just might be the world's fastest dip—and it's full of fiber, protein and flavor. Any white bean will do, so it's versatile to boot. Make it a few hours before serving so the flavors can really develop; then serve it with crisp fresh veggies.

One 19-ounce can white beans, rinsed and drained

⅓ cup coarsely chopped basil

3 tablespoons fresh lemon juice

1 tablespoon + 1 teaspoon extra virgin olive oil

1 large garlic clove

½ teaspoon salt

In a blender or food processor, puree the beans, basil, lemon juice, oil, garlic and salt. Let stand at room temperature, covered, until the flavors are blended, 2–3 hours.

serving provides: 2 Protein/Milks, 1 Fat.

per serving: 193 Calories, 5 g Total Fat, 1 g Saturated Fat, 0 mg Cholesterol, 643 mg Sodium, 28 g Total Carbohydrate, 7 g Dietary Fiber, 10 g Protein, 70 mg Calcium.

POINTS per serving: 3.

hint
Integrate beans (like kidney, black and pinto) into your favorite main dishes. Stir white beans into pasta, use mashed chickpeas as a sandwich filling or add beans to your salad at the salad bar. One-half cup of most beans contains about 6–8 grams of fiber.

make ahead

Vegetable Pâté

makes 8 servings

*This earthy, rich pâté is perfect for serving to company to spread on crackers.
Your guests will never suspect how easy it is to prepare. If there is any left over,
it also makes a great filling for sandwiches.*

2 teaspoons vegetable oil

2 onions, finely chopped

1½ cups finely chopped mushrooms

2 cups chopped steamed green beans

½ cup chopped walnuts

¼ cup chopped flat-leaf parsley

2 teaspoons chopped sage

½ teaspoon ground allspice

½ teaspoon salt

¼ teaspoon freshly ground black
pepper

6 ounces Pressed Tofu (page 8),
coarsely shredded

1. In a medium nonstick skillet, heat the oil. Add the onions; cook, stirring as needed, until softened, about 5 minutes. Add the mushrooms; cook, stirring as needed, until wilted, about 5 minutes. Add the beans and walnuts; cook, stirring, until the nuts are toasted, 2–3 minutes.

2. Transfer the mixture to a food processor. Add the parsley, sage, allspice, salt and pepper; pulse until fairly smooth. Transfer the mixture to a medium bowl. Squeeze the tofu to remove any excess moisture; add to the mixture. Refrigerate, covered, until chilled, at least 2 hours.

serving provides: 1 Fruit/Vegetable, 1 Fat.

per serving: 106 Calories, 7 g Total Fat, 0 g Saturated Fat, 0 mg Cholesterol, 150 mg Sodium, 8 g Total Carbohydrate, 3 g Dietary Fiber, 6 g Protein, 41 mg Calcium.

POINTS per serving: 2.

make ahead

one pot

Chunky Guacamole

makes 8 servings

We add lots of fresh vegetables and zippy spices to make this guacamole higher in flavor and lighter in fat. If you prefer milder guacamole, use just one jalapeño—or none at all. Serve it with baked tortilla chips or fresh vegetables at your next fiesta.

1 medium avocado, peeled and diced

2 tomatoes, diced

½ red bell pepper, seeded and diced

½ cucumber, diced

1 red onion, diced

2 tablespoons fresh lime juice

2 jalapeño peppers, seeded, deveined and minced (wear gloves to prevent irritation)

2 garlic cloves, minced

2 tablespoons chopped cilantro

½ teaspoon salt

½ teaspoon freshly ground black pepper

In a large bowl, combine the avocado, tomatoes, bell pepper, cucumber, onion, lime juice, jalapeños, garlic, cilantro, salt and pepper. Serve at once or refrigerate, covered, up to 2 days.

serving provides: 1 Fruit/Vegetable, 1 Fat.

per serving: 53 Calories, 4 g Total Fat, 0 g Saturated Fat, 0 mg Cholesterol, 164 mg Sodium, 4 g Total Carbohydrate, 4 g Dietary Fiber, 1 g Protein, 18 mg Calcium.

POINTS **per serving:** 1.

hint
Instead of cold cuts or tuna salad for lunch, try spreads like guacamole or hummus, roasted vegetables in sandwiches, or have a veggie burger. Pasta salads are another great vegetarian option.

make ahead

rush hour

Tomato-Herb Yogurt Cheese

makes 4 servings

This tasty spread will become a staple in your refrigerator. Spread it on toasted Italian bread for a light lunch, or serve it as a dip for cut-up veggies or savory whole-grain crackers—have fun discovering your favorite way to eat it.

4 sun-dried tomato halves (not oil-packed)

1 cup Yogurt Cheese (page 4)

¼ cup chopped basil

1 garlic clove, crushed

½ teaspoon minced thyme

¼ teaspoon salt

¼ teaspoon freshly ground black pepper

1. In a small bowl, soak the tomatoes in warm water until pliable, about 10 minutes. Drain and chop the tomatoes.

2. In the small bowl, combine the tomatoes, Yogurt Cheese, basil, garlic and thyme. Refrigerate, covered, until chilled, at least 1 hour. Stir well before serving.

serving provides: 1 Fruit/Vegetable.

per serving: 55 Calories, 0 g Total Fat, 0 g Saturated Fat, 2 mg Cholesterol, 239 mg Sodium, 7 g Total Carbohydrate, 0 g Dietary Fiber, 6 g Protein, 171 mg Calcium.

POINTS per serving: 1.

hint
Looking for foods with big flavor and little fat? Try blue, feta or extra-sharp cheddar cheeses; roasted peppers; sun-dried tomatoes; and fresh or dried wild mushrooms. Add to omelets, salads or plain pasta.

make ahead

Roasted Red Pepper Hummus

makes 4 servings

This dip is super-quick—and super-tasty—made with jarred roasted red peppers, but it is superb with freshly roasted ones. Next time you roast a bunch of peppers, add an extra one to use in this dip. Serve it with vegetable sticks or whole-wheat pita triangles.

One 15-ounce can chickpeas, rinsed and drained

½ cup drained roasted red peppers, or ½ medium red bell pepper, roasted★

2 tablespoons chopped flat-leaf parsley

2 tablespoons fresh lemon juice

2 tablespoons tahini (sesame paste)

1–2 garlic cloves, chopped

½ teaspoon salt

In a blender or food processor, puree the chickpeas, peppers, parsley, lemon juice, tahini, garlic and salt. Refrigerate, covered, until chilled, at least 1 hour.

serving provides: 2 Protein/Milks.

per serving: 144 Calories, 6 g Total Fat, 0 g Saturated Fat, 0 mg Cholesterol, 395 mg Sodium, 15 g Total Carbohydrate, 5 g Dietary Fiber, 7 g Protein, 38 mg Calcium.

POINTS per serving: 2.

make ahead

★ To roast bell pepper, preheat broiler. Line baking sheet with foil; place pepper on baking sheet. Broil 4–6" from heat, turning frequently with tongs, until skin is lightly charred on all sides, about 10 minutes. Transfer to paper bag; fold bag closed and let steam 10 minutes. Peel, seed and devein pepper over sink to drain juices.

Pinto Bean Quesadillas

makes 4 servings

These easy quesadillas will be a hit with everyone in the house. If you like them really spicy, add some extra jalapeños. Feel free to experiment using different kinds of beans, too.

One 19-ounce can pinto beans, rinsed and drained

1 jalapeño pepper, seeded, deveined and minced (wear gloves to prevent irritation)

1 tablespoon cider vinegar

Four 6" flour tortillas

¼ cup shredded extra-sharp cheddar cheese

1 tomato, thinly sliced

2 garlic cloves, minced

½ teaspoon freshly ground black pepper

1. In a blender or food processor, puree the beans, jalapeño and vinegar.

2. Spread the bean mixture over the tortillas and sprinkle with the cheese. Arrange the tomato slices over one side of each tortilla; sprinkle with the garlic and pepper. Fold the tortillas in half, pressing flat.

3. In a small nonstick skillet, heat the tortillas, one at a time, pressing down with a spatula, until golden, about 2 minutes on each side. Cut into triangles.

serving provides: 1 Bread, 2 Protein/Milks.

per serving: 250 Calories, 6 g Total Fat, 2 g Saturated Fat, 10 mg Cholesterol, 527 mg Sodium, 38 g Total Carbohydrate, 6 g Dietary Fiber, 11 g Protein, 162 mg Calcium.

POINTS per serving: 4.

one pot

rush hour

spicy

chapter three

ENTRÉES

Vegetarian Fajitas

makes 4 servings

This dish is not only quick, easy and tasty, but it's fun to make as well. Let everybody roll their own fajitas right at the table. Make the vegetables a day ahead, and reheat them just before serving.

1 tablespoon + 1 teaspoon olive oil

2 green bell peppers, seeded and cut into strips

2 onions, thinly sliced

1 medium zucchini, sliced

1 medium yellow squash, sliced

2 jalapeño peppers, seeded, deveined and minced (wear gloves to prevent irritation)

4 garlic cloves, minced

½ teaspoon salt

¼ teaspoon freshly ground black pepper

One 16-ounce can fat-free refried beans

4 cups finely shredded iceberg lettuce

½ cup fat-free salsa

½ cup nonfat sour cream

Eight 6" flour tortillas

1. In a large nonstick skillet, heat the oil. Add the bell peppers, onions, zucchini, squash, jalapeños, garlic, salt and pepper; cook, stirring as needed, until the vegetables are very soft, 15–20 minutes.

2. In the microwave or a small saucepan, heat the refried beans. Place the vegetables, beans, lettuce, salsa and sour cream in bowls; arrange on the serving table. Place two tortillas on each of four plates and serve, allowing each person to fill and roll their own fajitas.

serving provides: 2 Breads, 3 Fruit/Vegetables, 2 Protein/Milks, 1 Fat.

per serving: 459 Calories, 10 g Total Fat, 1 g Saturated Fat, 0 mg Cholesterol, 1177 mg Sodium, 78 g Total Carbohydrate, 9 g Dietary Fiber, 16 g Protein, 202 mg Calcium.

POINTS **per serving:** 8.

make ahead

microwave

spicy

Broccoli Rabe and Rice Frittata

makes 6 servings

Broccoli rabe is an intense, somewhat bitter green popular in Italian and Chinese cooking. It is high in vitamins yet low in calories and adds a wonderful sharp taste to this frittata. When you broil the frittata, keep the broiler door ajar with the handle of the skillet sticking out to avoid melting it or burning yourself.

2 teaspoons olive oil

2 onions, chopped

2½ cups chopped cleaned broccoli rabe

3 garlic cloves, minced

½ teaspoon crushed red pepper flakes

½ teaspoon fennel seeds

1½ cups Perfect Brown Rice (page 12)

6 eggs

3 egg whites

½ cup grated Parmesan cheese

½ teaspoon freshly ground black pepper

½ teaspoon salt

1. Preheat the broiler. In a large nonstick skillet with an ovenproof handle, heat the oil, tilting the pan so that the oil covers the sides. Add the onions; cook, stirring as needed, until softened, about 5 minutes. Add the broccoli rabe, garlic, pepper flakes and fennel seeds; cook until the broccoli rabe is wilted, about 3 minutes. Add the rice; toss to combine.

2. In a medium bowl, combine the eggs, egg whites, cheese, pepper and salt. Pour the egg mixture over the rice mixture and smooth over with a spatula. Reduce the heat to low; cook, lifting the sides of the frittata to allow the egg mixture to run underneath, until the eggs are almost set, about 10 minutes. Broil the frittata until the egg mixture is set and the top is golden, 2–3 minutes (keep the handle of the skillet out of the broiler to avoid melting it or burning yourself). Slide the frittata onto a plate and cut into 6 wedges.

serving provides: 1 Bread, 1 Fruit/Vegetable, 2 Protein/Milks.

per serving: 211 Calories, 9 g Total Fat, 3 g Saturated Fat, 217 mg Cholesterol, 423 mg Sodium, 18 g Total Carbohydrate, 3 g Dietary Fiber, 14 g Protein, 155 mg Calcium.

POINTS per serving: 4.

one pot

Spanish Tortilla

This tortilla is nothing like the Mexican flatbread. In Spain, "tortilla" refers to a thin omelet; it is a classic Spanish dish.

2 teaspoons olive oil

4 onions, chopped

1 green bell pepper, seeded and chopped

4 large all-purpose potatoes, cooked and cubed

3 garlic cloves, minced

6 eggs

3 egg whites

½ teaspoon freshly ground black pepper

½ teaspoon salt

1. Preheat the broiler. In a large nonstick skillet with an ovenproof handle, heat the oil, tilting the pan so that the oil covers the sides. Add the onions and bell pepper; cook, stirring as needed, until softened, 7–8 minutes. Add the potatoes and garlic; cook, stirring as needed, until the potatoes are browned, about 5 minutes.

2. In a medium bowl, combine the eggs, egg whites, pepper and salt. Pour the egg mixture over the potatoes and smooth over with a spatula. Reduce the heat to low; cook, lifting the sides of the tortilla to allow the egg mixture to run underneath, until the egg is almost set, about 10 minutes. Broil the tortilla until the egg mixture is set and the top is golden, 2–3 minutes (keep the handle of the skillet out of the broiler to avoid melting it or burning yourself). Slide the tortilla onto a plate and cut into 6 wedges.

serving provides: 1 Bread, 1 Fruit/Vegetable, 1 Protein/Milk.

per serving: 280 Calories, 7 g Total Fat, 2 g Saturated Fat, 212 mg Cholesterol, 296 mg Sodium, 43 g Total Carbohydrate, 4 g Dietary Fiber, 12 g Protein, 58 mg Calcium.

POINTS per serving: 5.

one pot

Polenta-Stuffed Peppers

makes 4 servings

This unusual pepper filling is rich and tasty. You can serve it as a side dish by itself.

4 red bell peppers

2 teaspoons olive oil

1 onion, diced

1 medium zucchini, diced

3 garlic cloves, minced

½ cup instant polenta

1 tomato, diced

¼ cup grated Parmesan cheese

¼ cup chopped flat-leaf parsley

1. Preheat the oven to 375°F. Spray an 8" square baking dish with nonstick cooking spray. Cut the tops off the peppers about ¼" below the stems, then scoop out the seeds and veins.

2. In a medium saucepan, heat the oil. Add the onion; cook, stirring as needed, until softened, about 5 minutes. Add the zucchini and garlic; cook, stirring as needed, until softened, about 5 minutes. Add 2 cups water and bring to a boil. Slowly stir in the polenta; cook, stirring constantly, until thickened, about 5 minutes. Stir in the tomato, cheese and parsley.

3. Spoon the polenta mixture into the peppers. Place peppers in the baking dish; bake until the peppers are tender and the polenta is golden, about 30 minutes.

serving provides: 2 Breads, 2 Fruit/Vegetables, 1 Fat.

per serving: 157 Calories, 4 g Total Fat, 1 g Saturated Fat, 4 mg Cholesterol, 103 mg Sodium, 25 g Total Carbohydrate, 5 g Dietary Fiber, 6 g Protein, 105 mg Calcium.

POINTS per serving: 2.

hint
A light salad always fits into a meal: Chicory (also called frisée or curly endive) is a lettuce-like green with firm, curly leaves and has a slightly bitter flavor. It works well with rich main courses or in a salad with a sweet-and-sour dressing.

Indian Split Pea and Vegetable Cake

This traditional Indian cake is perfect with mango chutney or a fruit-sweetened salsa.

1 cup boiling water

½ cup bulgur

1 cup yellow split peas, picked over, rinsed and drained

2 tablespoons grated peeled ginger-root

3 garlic cloves, minced

½ teaspoon ground cumin

¼ teaspoon ground cardamom

¼ teaspoon cayenne pepper

2 teaspoons vegetable oil

2 medium onions, sliced

4 cups sliced mushrooms

4 serrano chiles, seeded, deveined and sliced (wear gloves to prevent irritation)

¼ cup minced cilantro

¼ cup orange juice

1. In a small bowl, combine the water and bulgur. Let stand, covered, until soft, about 30 minutes.

2. In a medium saucepan, combine the peas, ginger, garlic, cumin, cardamom, cayenne and 2 cups water; bring to a boil. Reduce the heat and simmer until the peas are tender, about 30 minutes; drain any excess water. Transfer to a blender or food processor and pulse until fairly smooth.

3. Preheat the oven to 400°F. Spray a 9" springform pan with nonstick cooking spray.

4. In a medium nonstick skillet, heat the oil. Add the onions; cook, stirring as needed, until softened, about 5 minutes. Add the mushrooms; cook, stirring as needed, until golden, about 10 minutes. Add the chiles; cook, stirring, 1 minute.

5. Transfer the mushroom mixture to a large bowl. Add the bulgur, pea mixture, cilantro and orange juice; combine. Transfer to the pan. Bake until firm, 45–50 minutes. Let stand 10 minutes before cutting into 6 wedges.

serving provides: 1 Bread, 1 Fruit/Vegetable, 1 Protein/Milk.

per serving: 206 Calories, 2 g Total Fat, 0 g Saturated Fat, 0 mg Cholesterol, 57 mg Sodium, 37 g Total Carbohydrate, 12 g Dietary Fiber, 11 g Protein, 52 mg Calcium.

POINTS per serving: 2.

make ahead

Good Advice

Looking for ideas on how to get your daily quota of 20 to 25 grams of fiber? Consider this list:

1. ¾ cup raisin bran (5 grams)

    2. 1 red apple (3 grams)

3. 2 slices whole-wheat bread (3.2 grams)

    4. lettuce and tomato garnish (.5 grams)

5. 1 cup air-popped popcorn (1.3 grams)

    6. 1 cup spinach salad (1.4 grams)

7. 1 pear (4.3 grams)

    8. 1 cup cooked long-grain brown rice (3.3 grams)

9. 1 cup cooked carrots (3 grams)

    10. 1 kiwi fruit (3.1 grams)

Swiss Chard–Ricotta Torta

makes 4 servings

If you can't find fresh Swiss chard, substitute spinach, kale or beet greens.

¼ cup plain dried bread crumbs

2 teaspoons olive oil

2 onions, chopped

1 bunch Swiss chard, cleaned and chopped

3 garlic cloves, minced

1 cup part-skim ricotta cheese

2 eggs, lightly beaten

½ teaspoon salt

¼ teaspoon freshly ground black pepper

1. Preheat the oven to 400°F. Spray a 9" springform pan with nonstick cooking spray; sprinkle with 2 tablespoons of the bread crumbs.

2. In a large nonstick skillet, heat the oil. Add the onions; cook, stirring as needed, until softened, about 5 minutes. Stir in the chard and garlic; cook, stirring as needed, until the chard is tender, about 5 minutes.

3. Meanwhile, in a medium bowl, combine the ricotta, eggs, salt, pepper and the remaining 2 tablespoons of bread crumbs; stir in the chard mixture, then spoon into the pan. Bake until puffed, golden and firm to the touch, 45–50 minutes. Let stand 10 minutes before cutting into 4 wedges.

serving provides: 2 Fruit/Vegetables, 1 Protein/Milk, 1 Fat.

per serving: 235 Calories, 10 g Total Fat, 4 g Saturated Fat, 125 mg Cholesterol, 801 mg Sodium, 22 g Total Carbohydrate, 5 g Dietary Fiber, 15 g Protein, 326 mg Calcium.

POINTS per serving: 5.

White Bean Risotto with Fragrant Herbs

makes 4 servings

Fennel and tarragon subtly infuse this risotto with the fragrance and flavor of anise. It makes a wonderful lunch served with a mixed green salad. Use any small white bean—great Northern or navy beans are good. Top with shavings of Parmesan, if you like.

5 cups Vegetable Broth (page 2)

1 tablespoons + 1 teaspoon olive oil

½ fennel bulb, chopped

1 onion, chopped

1⅓ cups Arborio rice

One 19-ounce can small white beans, rinsed and drained

½ cup chopped flat-leaf parsley

2 tablespoons fresh lemon juice

2 teaspoons minced tarragon

½ teaspoon freshly ground black pepper

1. In a medium saucepan, bring the broth to a boil. Reduce the heat and simmer.

2. In a medium nonstick saucepan, heat the oil. Add the fennel and onion; cook, stirring as needed, until softened, about 5 minutes. Add the rice; cook, stirring to coat, about 1 minute.

3. Add 1 cup of the broth; cook, stirring, until the broth is absorbed. Add 1 more cup of the broth; cook, stirring, until the broth is absorbed. Continue adding broth, ½ cup at a time, stirring, while the broth is absorbed, until the rice is just tender; add the beans with the last addition of broth. The total cooking time should be about 25–30 minutes. Stir in the parsley, lemon juice, tarragon and pepper; serve at once.

serving provides: 2 Breads, 2 Protein/Milks, 1 Fat.

per serving: 469 Calories, 6 g Total Fat, 1 g Saturated Fat, 0 mg Cholesterol, 426 mg Sodium, 90 g Total Carbohydrate, 8 g Dietary Fiber, 15 g Protein, 90 mg Calcium.

POINTS **per serving:** 8.

hint
Baffled by fennel? Enjoy its strong licorice flavor tossed into salads (simply cut it into thin strips or dice), sautéed (place in a nonstick pan over medium heat and sauté slowly, about 15 minutes), or raw (it's purported to be an after-dinner digestive).

(See photo insert.)

Risotto with Artichokes and Leeks

makes 4 servings

The tricks to making creamy risotto are to keep the rice cooking at a low boil and to stir with a flat-edged wooden spatula so that you can get into the edge of the pot to keep the rice moving.

4 cups Vegetable Broth (page 2)

Two 10-ounce packages frozen artichoke hearts, thawed

1 tablespoon + 1 teaspoon olive oil

2 leeks, cleaned and thinly sliced

1 cup Arborio rice

⅓ cup grated Parmesan cheese

1 teaspoon minced rosemary

1. In a medium saucepan, bring the broth to a boil. Reduce the heat and simmer.

2. Cut the artichoke hearts into quarters; set aside.

3. In a medium nonstick saucepan, heat the oil. Add the leeks; cook, stirring as needed, until softened, about 5 minutes. Add the rice; cook, stirring to coat, about 1 minute.

4. Add 1 cup of the broth; cook, stirring, until the broth is absorbed. Add ½ cup of the broth; cook, stirring, until the broth is absorbed. Continue adding broth, ½ cup at a time, stirring while the broth is absorbed, until the rice is just tender; add the artichokes with the last addition of broth. The total cooking time should be about 25–30 minutes. Stir in the cheese and rosemary; serve at once.

serving provides: 2 Breads, 2 Fruit/Vegetables, 1 Protein/Milk, 1 Fat.

per serving: 366 Calories, 8 g Total Fat, 2 g Saturated Fat, 5 mg Cholesterol, 287 mg Sodium, 65 g Total Carbohydrate, 2 g Dietary Fiber, 12 g Protein, 141 mg Calcium.

POINTS per serving: 8.

Caribbean Cowpeas and Rice

makes 4 servings

Variations of peas and rice are served all over the Caribbean. Serve this one with a few drops of your favorite hot sauce and some lemon wedges. Cowpeas are small, light tan beans with brown "eyes"; if you can't find them, use black-eyed peas or pigeon peas.

1 cup cowpeas, picked over, rinsed and drained

1 onion, chopped

2 jalapeño peppers, seeded, deveined and minced (wear gloves to prevent irritation)

2 garlic cloves, minced

½ teaspoon ground cumin

½ teaspoon dried thyme

1 bay leaf

1 cup long-grain white rice

1 cup Vegetable Broth (page 2)

½ cup canned crushed tomatoes (no salt added)

½ teaspoon ground allspice

½ teaspoon salt

1. Soak the cowpeas (see page 5).

2. In a medium saucepan, combine the cowpeas, onion, jalapeños, garlic, cumin, thyme, bay leaf and 2 cups water; bring to a boil. Reduce the heat and simmer until the cowpeas are tender, about 25 minutes.

3. Stir in the rice, broth, tomatoes, allspice and salt; bring to a boil. Reduce the heat and simmer, covered, until the liquid is absorbed, about 20 minutes; discard the bay leaf.

serving provides: 2 Breads, 2 Protein/Milks.

per serving: 295 Calories, 2 g Total Fat, 0 g Saturated Fat, 0 mg Cholesterol, 339 mg Sodium 59 g Total Carbohydrate, 9 g Dietary Fiber, 11 g Protein, 62 mg Calcium.

POINTS per serving: 4.

hint
Keep cut-up vegetables, such as carrot sticks, broccoli, peppers and celery, in sealed, zip-closed plastic bags or airtight, lidded containers. Make sure they're thoroughly dried before storing (sealing them wet encourages mold).

make ahead

one pot

spicy

Black Bean Tostadas

makes 4 servings

Make the bean mixture a day or two ahead—it gives the flavors time to blend, and it simplifies getting dinner on the table.

Four 6" corn tortillas

2 teaspoons vegetable oil

1 onion, chopped

One 19-ounce can black beans, rinsed and drained

1 tomato, diced

1 tablespoon dried currants

1 tablespoon red-wine vinegar

2 garlic cloves, minced

1 teaspoon chili powder

2 cups shredded iceberg lettuce

½ medium avocado, peeled and diced

¼ cup salsa

¼ cup nonfat sour cream

1. Preheat the oven to 350°F. Place the tortillas on a baking sheet; bake, turning frequently, until golden and crisp, about 8 minutes.

2. In a medium nonstick skillet, heat the oil. Add the onion; cook, stirring as needed, until softened, about 5 minutes. Add the beans, tomato, currants, vinegar, garlic and chili powder; cook, mashing the beans with the back of a wooden spoon, about 10 minutes.

3. Spread the bean mixture over the tortillas; layer with the lettuce, avocado, salsa and sour cream.

serving provides: 1 Bread, 1 Fruit/Vegetable, 2 Protein/Milks, 2 Fats.

per serving: 258 Calories, 8 g Total Fat, 0 g Saturated Fat, 0 mg Cholesterol, 344 mg Sodium, 40 g Total Carbohydrate, 13 g Dietary Fiber, 10 g Protein, 118 mg Calcium.

POINTS **per serving:** 6.

hint

Make your own fat-free taco shells by hanging soft corn tortillas directly over the oven racks and baking at 400°F until crisp.

make ahead

rush hour

spicy

Rice and Chickpea–Stuffed Cabbage

makes 4 servings

This stuffed cabbage, made with brown rice and chickpeas, is even better the day after it is made. Bake it on a weekend, then reheat it for an easy midweek supper. Use the bagged sauerkraut from the deli case at your supermarket instead of the canned variety—it's not as salty (though it still should be rinsed) and its texture is crisper.

1 large green cabbage, cored

2 teaspoons vegetable oil

2 onions, chopped

One 15-ounce can chickpeas, rinsed, drained and chopped

1½ cups slightly undercooked Perfect Brown Rice (page 12)

¼ cup dried currants

½ teaspoon salt

½ teaspoon freshly ground black pepper

⅛ teaspoon dried marjoram or sage

1 cup Tomato Sauce (page 3)

1 cup sauerkraut, rinsed and squeezed dry

¼ cup minced dill

1 teaspoon sugar

1. Bring a large pot of water to a boil; add the cabbage, cored-end down, and simmer until the leaves are easily separated, 8–10 minutes. Run under cold water and drain. Carefully peel 8 large leaves from the cabbage; trim the outside edge of each leaf until it is pliable. Reserve the remaining cabbage for another use.

2. Preheat the oven to 350°F. In a medium nonstick skillet, heat the oil. Add the onions; cook, stirring as needed, until softened, about 5 minutes.

3. In a medium bowl, combine the chickpeas, rice, currants, salt, pepper and marjoram. Stir in the onions.

4. In a small saucepan, combine the Tomato Sauce, sauerkraut, dill, sugar and 1½ cups water; simmer 10 minutes. Pour a thin layer of sauce into a shallow 2- to 3-quart baking dish.

5. Place a cabbage leaf on a work surface. Place a generous ⅓ cup filling in the center, then fold in the sides and roll up. Place in the baking dish, seam-side down. Repeat with the remaining leaves and filling. Pour the remaining sauce over the cabbage rolls. Bake, covered loosely with foil, until the cabbage is tender and the sauce is thickened, 1½ hours. Let stand 30 minutes; then serve with any remaining sauce on the side.

serving provides: 1 Bread, 2 Fruit/Vegetables, 1 Protein/Milk, 1 Fat.

per serving: 303 Calories, 5 g Total Fat, 1 g Saturated Fat, 0 mg Cholesterol, 860 mg Sodium, 56 g Total Carbohydrate, 10 g Dietary Fiber, 11 g Protein, 162 mg Calcium.

POINTS **per serving:** 4.

hint
For a traditional Eastern European salad, thinly slice some cucumbers and an onion and toss with distilled white vinegar, dill and a dash of sugar.

make ahead

Bulgur-Stuffed Mushrooms

makes 4 servings

Double the mushrooms make these doubly delicious. If dried porcini mushrooms are not available, or you want a less-intense mushroom flavor, omit the porcinis and plump the bulgur with boiling water.

One .35-ounce package dried porcini mushrooms

½ cup bulgur

12 large white mushrooms

1 tablespoon + 1 teaspoon vegetable oil

3 garlic cloves, minced

¼ cup chopped flat-leaf parsley

1 egg, lightly beaten

2 tablespoons chopped basil

¼ teaspoon salt

¼ teaspoon freshly ground black pepper

Pinch dried marjoram

2 tablespoons grated Parmesan cheese

1. Preheat the oven to 400°F. Spray a 13x9" baking dish with nonstick cooking spray. In a small bowl, combine the porcinis and 1 cup warm water; let soak 10 minutes. Set a paper towel–lined strainer over a small saucepan; pour the soaking liquid through the strainer. Rinse the porcinis, then chop them and set aside.

2. In the microwave, bring the soaking liquid to a boil. Remove from the heat, add the bulgur and let stand, covered, until the bulgur is soft, about 30 minutes.

3. Remove the stems from the white mushrooms; brush the caps with 2 teaspoons of the oil, then chop the stems. In a medium nonstick skillet, heat the remaining 2 teaspoons of the oil. Add the stems and garlic; cook, stirring as needed, until golden, 7–8 minutes. Stir in the bulgur, porcinis, parsley, egg, basil, salt, pepper and marjoram.

4. Stuff the mushroom caps with the filling and place in the baking dish. Bake until heated through, about 20 minutes; sprinkle with the cheese and bake until the cheese is melted, about 5 minutes longer.

serving provides: 1 Bread, 1 Fruit/Vegetable, 1 Fat.

per serving: 146 Calories, 7 g Total Fat, 2 g Saturated Fat, 55 mg Cholesterol, 214 mg Sodium, 17 g Total Carbohydrate, 4 g Dietary Fiber, 5 g Protein, 59 mg Calcium.

POINTS per serving: 3.

microwave

Spinach Pie

makes 4 servings

Based on the traditional Greek dish spanakopita, our interpretation will make a spinach lover out of anyone. Make sure that the spinach is washed very well, or use two 10-ounce packages of frozen chopped spinach.

2 teaspoons olive oil

12 scallions, sliced

Two 10-ounce packages fresh spinach, cleaned and coarsely chopped

¾ cup crumbled feta cheese

⅔ cup low-fat cottage cheese

½ cup minced dill

2 eggs, lightly beaten

¼ teaspoon freshly ground black pepper

6 sheets phyllo dough, thawed if frozen

1. Preheat the oven to 350°F. Spray an 8" square baking pan with nonstick cooking spray. In a medium nonstick skillet, heat the oil. Add the scallions; cook, stirring, 1 minute.

Add the spinach; cook, stirring as needed, until just wilted, 3–5 minutes. Transfer to a medium bowl; stir in the cheeses, dill, eggs and pepper.

2. Spray 1 phyllo sheet with nonstick cooking spray; top with another sheet and spray it. Line the baking pan with these 2 sheets, letting the edges hang over the sides. Spread the spinach mixture over the phyllo. Cover the filling with the remaining 4 sheets, spraying each sheet and tucking them into the pan. Fold in the outside sheets. Bake until golden, 30–35 minutes.

serving provides: 1 Bread, 4 Fruit/Vegetables, 1 Protein/Milk, 1 Fat.

per serving: 264 Calories, 12 g Total Fat, 5 g Saturated Fat, 127 mg Cholesterol, 676 mg Sodium, 24 g Total Carbohydrate, 4 g Dietary Fiber, 17 g Protein, 299 mg Calcium.

POINTS per serving: 5.

hint
Make your own nonstick spray: Fill a plastic plant mister (sold in five-and-ten stores) with olive oil. For a gourmet touch, add dried herbs, such as oregano, basil, rosemary or thyme.

(See photo insert.)

Layered Vegetable Terrine

makes 4 servings

If you like ratatouille, you will love this terrine. It is best made a few hours ahead so that the flavors have a chance to blend. Serve with some nice crusty bread.

1 medium (1¼-pound) eggplant, cut into ⅜" slices

¾ teaspoon salt

4 medium zucchini, thinly sliced lengthwise

1 tablespoon + 1 teaspoon olive oil

3 red bell peppers, roasted★

6 sun-dried tomato halves (not oil-packed), chopped

½ cup chopped flat-leaf parsley

¼ cup grated Parmesan cheese

4 garlic cloves, minced

1 teaspoon grated lemon zest

½ teaspoon freshly ground black pepper

1. Preheat the broiler. Place the eggplant on paper towels and sprinkle with ½ teaspoon of the salt. Cover with a plate and press for 20 minutes. Rinse and squeeze dry between more paper towels.

2. In a medium bowl, toss the eggplant and zucchini with the oil; arrange in a single layer on nonstick baking sheets. Broil until lightly browned, 3–4 minutes on each side.

3. Reduce the oven temperature to 350°F. Spray a loaf pan with nonstick cooking spray. In a small bowl, combine the tomatoes, parsley, cheese, garlic, lemon zest, pepper and the remaining ¼ teaspoon of the salt. In the loaf pan, layer one-third of the peppers, one-half of the eggplant, and one-half of the zucchini, sprinkling the parsley mixture between each layer. Repeat the layers, finishing with the peppers. Bake, covered with foil, 40 minutes. Uncover and bake until the vegetables are tender, about 25 minutes longer. Let stand 10 minutes before cutting into 4 slices.

serving provides: 3 Fruit/Vegetables, 1 Fat.

per serving: 148 Calories, 7 g Total Fat, 2 g Saturated Fat, 4 mg Cholesterol, 306 mg Sodium, 19 g Total Carbohydrate, 8 g Dietary Fiber, 7 g Protein, 127 mg Calcium.

POINTS per serving: 2.

★To roast bell peppers, preheat broiler. Line baking sheet with foil; place peppers on baking sheet. Broil 4–6" from heat, turning frequently with tongs, until skin is lightly charred on all sides, about 10 minutes. Transfer to paper bag; fold bag closed and let steam 10 minutes. Peel, seed and devein peppers over sink to drain juices.

make ahead

Veggie Paella

makes 4 servings

Spanish medium- or short-grain rice works best for this dish. Look for it in the Spanish-foods section of most supermarkets.

1¾ cups Vegetable Broth (page 2)

1–2 pinches saffron threads

1 tablespoon olive oil

1 onion, chopped

1½ cups medium- or short-grain white rice

3 garlic cloves, minced

1 cup canned diced tomatoes (no salt added)

1 cup drained rinsed canned cannellini beans

6 large black olives, pitted and sliced

2 tablespoons drained rinsed capers

2 teaspoons minced thyme

½ teaspoon salt

¼ teaspoon freshly ground black pepper

1 red bell pepper, seeded and cut into 1" squares

1 green bell pepper, seeded and cut in 1" squares

1. Preheat the oven to 350°F. In a small saucepan, bring the broth to a boil. Remove from the heat, add the saffron and let stand 10 minutes.

2. In a paella pan or large nonstick skillet, heat the oil. Add the onion; cook, stirring as needed, until softened, about 5 minutes. Add the rice and garlic; cook, stirring, about 1 minute.

3. Stir in the broth and tomatoes; bring to a boil and boil 1 minute. Remove from the heat and stir in the beans, olives, capers, thyme, salt and pepper. Scatter the bell peppers on top. Bake until the rice is just tender, 15–17 minutes. Cover and let stand 10 minutes before serving.

serving provides: 2 Breads, 1 Fruit/Vegetable, 1 Protein/Milk, 1 Fat.

per serving: 231 Calories, 5 g Total Fat, 1 g Saturated Fat, 0 mg Cholesterol, 977 mg Sodium, 41 g Total Carbohydrate, 7 g Dietary Fiber, 7 g Protein, 59 mg Calcium.
POINTS **per serving:** 4.

hint
Keep vegetables in the crisper drawer of the refrigerator, away from the fruit. As it ripens, fruit gives off a gas that can cause vegetables to spoil.

one pot

(See photo insert.)

chapter four

STIR–FRIES &
SKILLET MEALS

Vegetable and Quinoa Sauté with Orange

makes 4 servings

Although quinoa is new on restaurant menus, it's really not new at all—it was a staple in the diet of the ancient Incas. If you've never tried quinoa, this recipe is a fabulous introduction; it also makes a beautiful stuffing for acorn squash.

⅓ cup quinoa

2 teaspoons olive oil

1 onion, chopped

3 carrots, grated

2 garlic cloves, minced

½ teaspoon ground cumin

1 cup drained rinsed canned chickpeas

½ cup orange juice

¼ cup raisins

¼ teaspoon salt

⅛ teaspoon cinnamon

1 tablespoon chopped cilantro

1. Cook the quinoa according to package directions, either conventionally or in the microwave.

2. In a medium nonstick skillet, heat the oil. Add the onion; cook, stirring as needed, until softened, about 5 minutes. Add the carrots, garlic and cumin; cook, stirring as needed, until the carrots are wilted, about 2 minutes.

3. Stir in the quinoa, chickpeas, orange juice, raisins, salt and cinnamon; cook, covered, until the juice is absorbed and the flavors are blended, about 10 minutes. Stir in the cilantro.

serving provides: 1 Bread, 2 Fruit/Vegetables, 1 Protein/Milk, 1 Fat.

per serving: 205 Calories, 4 g Total Fat, 0 g Saturated Fat, 0 mg Cholesterol, 239 mg Sodium, 37 g Total Carbohydrate, 6 g Dietary Fiber, 6 g Protein, 62 mg Calcium.

POINTS per serving: 3.

make ahead

rush hour

microwave

Herbed Two Squash–Tempeh Sauté

makes 4 servings

*If you find the garden vegetable-flavored tempeh in your natural foods store,
try it in this easy dish.*

One ½-pound package tempeh, cubed

4 garlic cloves, minced

3 tablespoons reduced-sodium soy sauce

1 tablespoon + 1 teaspoon olive oil

2 onions, sliced

1 medium zucchini, halved lengthwise and sliced

1 medium yellow squash, halved lengthwise and sliced

2 tablespoons chopped flat-leaf parsley

2 tablespoons fresh lemon juice

½ teaspoon minced thyme

½ teaspoon minced rosemary

¼ teaspoon salt

¼ teaspoon freshly ground black pepper

1. In a medium saucepan, combine the tempeh, half of the garlic, the soy sauce and 2 cups water; bring to a boil. Reduce the heat and simmer 10 minutes. Drain and pat the tempeh dry.

2. In a large nonstick skillet, heat the oil. Add the onions, zucchini and squash; cook, stirring as needed, until the onions are softened, 5–6 minutes. Stir in the tempeh and the remaining garlic; cook, stirring as needed, until lightly browned, 2–3 minutes. Stir in the parsley, lemon juice, thyme, rosemary, salt and pepper; cook, covered, until the flavors are blended, 3–4 minutes.

serving provides: 1 Fruit/Vegetable, 2 Protein/Milks, 1 Fat.

per serving: 200 Calories, 9 g Total Fat, 1 g Saturated Fat, 0 mg Cholesterol, 604 mg Sodium, 17 g Total Carbohydrate, 6 g Dietary Fiber, 14 g Protein, 56 mg Calcium.

POINTS per serving: 4.

hint

Maximize the life of fresh herbs by placing them in a glass of water (as you would with a bouquet of flowers) and covering loosely with a plastic bag (the one you put them in at the grocery store is perfect); refrigerate and change the water daily.

rush hour

Potato and Broccoli Rabe Skillet Pie

makes 4 servings

As the pie cooks, shake the pan occasionally so that the potatoes do not stick. If they do, the dish will be just as tasty, but it may need patching when you invert it.

hint

Top baked potatoes with plain nonfat yogurt, instead of sour cream, before you sprinkle with chives.

1 tablespoon + 1 teaspoon olive oil

1 onion, sliced

1 bunch broccoli rabe, cleaned and coarsely chopped

2 garlic cloves, minced

½ teaspoon fennel seeds

4 small all-purpose potatoes, peeled and thinly sliced

½ teaspoon salt

¼ teaspoon freshly ground black pepper

1. In a large nonstick skillet, heat 2 teaspoons of the oil. Add the onion; cook, stirring as needed, until softened, about 5 minutes. Add the broccoli rabe, garlic and fennel seeds; cook, stirring as needed, until the broccoli rabe is wilted, about 5 minutes. Transfer to a plate; wipe out the skillet with paper towels.

2. Add the remaining 2 teaspoons of the oil to the skillet. Arrange half the potato slices in the bottom of the skillet, overlapping if necessary. Sprinkle with ¼ teaspoon of the salt and ⅛ teaspoon of the pepper. Spoon the broccoli rabe over the potatoes. Cover with the remaining potatoes; sprinkle with the remaining ¼ teaspoon of the salt and ⅛ teaspoon of the pepper. Cover the potatoes with a heat-proof plate to weight them down. Reduce the heat; cook, covered, until the potatoes are cooked through and the bottoms are browned, 40–45 minutes. Invert onto a serving platter.

serving provides: 1 Bread, 2 Fruit/Vegetables, 1 Fat.

per serving: 175 Calories, 5 g Total Fat, 1 g Saturated Fat, 0 mg Cholesterol, 336 mg Sodium, 29 g Total Carbohydrate, 6 g Dietary Fiber, 7 g Protein, 83 mg Calcium.

POINTS per serving: 3.

one pot

Scrambled Tofu

makes 4 servings

This simple tofu dish is full of hearty vegetables. Stuff it in a whole-wheat pita for an easy lunch on the run.

1 tablespoon + 1 teaspoon olive oil

2 cups chopped mushrooms

1 red bell pepper, seeded and diced

8 scallions, sliced

1 garlic clove, minced

1 pound soft reduced-fat tofu, diced

½ teaspoon salt

¼ teaspoon freshly ground black pepper

2 tablespoons chopped basil

2 tablespoons chopped flat-leaf parsley

1. In a large nonstick skillet, heat the oil. Add the mushrooms, bell pepper, scallions and garlic; cook, stirring as needed, until the vegetables are softened, 10–12 minutes.

2. Stir in the tofu, salt and pepper; cook, stirring as needed, until the tofu is heated through and the flavors are blended, about 5 minutes. Stir in the basil and parsley.

serving provides: 1 Fruit/Vegetable, 2 Protein/Milks, 1 Fat.

per serving: 128 Calories, 8 g Total Fat, 1 g Saturated Fat, 0 mg Cholesterol, 304 mg Sodium, 8 g Total Carbohydrate, 2 g Dietary Fiber, 7 g Protein, 47 mg Calcium.

POINTS **per serving:** 3.

one pot

rush hour

Good Advice

Here's how to work more soy into your diet:

1. Grill soy hot dogs and hamburgers for a quick weekday meal.

2. Blend soft tofu with sautéed onion, curry powder or roasted red peppers for a wonderful dip.

3. Substitute light soy milk for your regular milk. Soy milk, the liquid expressed from soaked and pureed soybeans, can be used as a milk substitute for coffee, cereal, baking and shakes, even drinking—try a flavored variety. It is sold in aseptic packaging in supermarkets and natural food stores and should be refrigerated after opening. Look for varieties fortified with vitamin D and calcium.

4. Try tempeh—a fermented, chunky cake of soybeans with a nutty flavor. It can be cubed and marinated with sauce and grilled, or crumbled and added to soups. Try tempeh burgers, kebobs (thread chunks of tempeh and green bell peppers) or a stir-fry (tossed with tamari sauce, broccoli, red peppers and mushrooms).

5. Consider adding TVP, or Textured Vegetable Protein, made from the flakes that remain after oil is extracted from soybeans, to casseroles, soups and stews. It's available in the dried-goods section of grocery and natural food stores. It adds a meaty flavor and texture to meatless favorites like chili and sloppy joes. In the frozen-foods section, you can find burgers, bacon, breakfast sausage and more—all made from TVP.

6. Replace up to one-fourth of the flour in muffins, quick breads and pancakes with soy flour.

7. Stretch your favorite meatloaf recipe (and make it healthier!) with ¾ cup grated Frozen Tofu (page 9). Or add some mashed soft tofu to macaroni and cheese.

8. Substitute Tofu Salad Dressing (page 5) for regular mayonnaise in salad dressings and on sandwiches.

9. Make a fruit shake with soy milk or tofu and frozen or fresh fruit. Blend 1 cup light soy milk or ½ cup silken tofu and ½ cup skim milk with 1 cup frozen peaches, strawberries or bananas. Add sweetener to taste.

Soy-Glazed Tofu Kale Sauté

makes 4 servings

*If you like kale, you will love this dish. Its assertive flavor seasons the tofu
perfectly and stands up deliciously to the soy sauce glaze.*

**1 tablespoons + 1 teaspoon vegetable
oil**

**1 pound Pressed Tofu (page 8),
cubed**

**1 bunch kale, cleaned and coarsely
chopped**

**1 tablespoon grated peeled ginger-
root**

3 garlic cloves, minced

**2 teaspoons reduced-sodium soy
sauce**

½ teaspoon Asian sesame oil

1. In a large nonstick skillet, heat 2 teaspoons
of the vegetable oil. Add the tofu; cook, stirring as needed, until golden, 5–6 minutes.
Transfer to a plate and keep warm.

2. In the same skillet, heat the remaining 2
teaspoons of the vegetable oil. Add the kale in
handfuls, stirring as it wilts. Add the ginger
and garlic; cook, stirring, 1 minute. Stir in
the soy sauce and ¼ cup water. Add the tofu;
cook, covered, until the tofu is glazed, about
5 minutes. Sprinkle with the sesame oil just
before serving.

serving provides: 2 Fruit/Vegetables, 2 Protein/
Milks, 1 Fat.

per serving: 229 Calories, 11 g Total Fat, 1 g
Saturated Fat, 0 mg Cholesterol, 156 mg Sodium,
18 g Total Carbohydrate, 9 g Dietary Fiber, 17 g
Protein, 206 mg Calcium.

POINTS **per serving:** 5.

one pot

rush hour

Vegetable Fried Rice

makes 4 servings

Everyone loves the Chinese-restaurant classic; our version leaves out the extra oil to make the most of the fresh flavors. Make sure the rice is cold—that way it won't clump.

1 tablespoon + 1 teaspoon vegetable oil

1 red bell pepper, seeded and finely diced

8 scallions, thinly sliced

3 cups cold Perfect Brown Rice (page 12)

2 teaspoons grated peeled gingerroot

2 eggs, lightly beaten

1 cup shredded Napa cabbage

⅓ pound green beans, steamed and cut into 1" lengths

1 tablespoon reduced-sodium soy sauce

1. In a medium nonstick skillet, heat the oil. Add the pepper and scallions; cook, stirring as needed, until the vegetables begin to soften, 2–3 minutes. Stir in the rice and ginger; cook, stirring as needed, until heated through, 5–6 minutes.

2. Push the rice mixture to the sides of the skillet; add the eggs to the center and cook, stirring constantly, until softly scrambled, about 1 minute. Continuing to stir, incorporate the rice. Stir in the cabbage, beans and soy sauce; cook, stirring constantly, until the cabbage is just wilted, 2–3 minutes.

serving provides: 2 Breads, 1 Fruit/Vegetable, 1 Fat.

per serving: 268 Calories, 8 g Total Fat, 1 g Saturated Fat, 106 mg Cholesterol, 192 mg Sodium, 42 g Total Carbohydrate, 4 g Dietary Fiber, 8 g Protein, 64 mg Calcium.

POINTS per serving: 5.

one pot

rush hour

Stir-Fried Tofu with Vegetables

makes 4 servings

Serve this with a mound of brown rice. If these vegetables are not your favorite, substitute whichever you like best.

1 tablespoon + 1 teaspoon vegetable oil

½ pound Pressed Tofu (page 8), cubed

4 carrots, sliced

1½ cups broccoli florets

½ cup sliced bamboo shoots

4 scallions, cut into 2" lengths

2 tablespoons grated peeled gingerroot

3 garlic cloves, thinly sliced

Pinch crushed hot pepper flakes

1 tablespoon reduced-sodium soy sauce

1 teaspoon sugar

1. In a large nonstick skillet, heat 1 tablespoon of the oil. Add the tofu; cook, stirring as needed, until golden, 5–6 minutes. Transfer to a plate and keep warm.

2. In the same skillet, heat the remaining 1 teaspoon of oil. Add the carrots, broccoli, bamboo shoots, scallions, ginger, garlic and pepper flakes; cook, stirring as needed, about 2 minutes.

3. In a small bowl, combine the soy sauce, sugar and ¼ cup water. Stir into the vegetable mixture, then add the tofu. Cook, covered, until most of the liquid is evaporated, about 10 minutes.

serving provides: 2 Fruit/Vegetables, 1 Protein/Milk, 1 Fat.

per serving: 154 Calories, 7 g Total Fat, 1 g Saturated Fat, 0 mg Cholesterol, 191 mg Sodium, 15 g Total Carbohydrate, 5 g Dietary Fiber, 9 g Protein, 73 mg Calcium.

POINTS per serving: 3.

hint
Keep a steady supply of precut broccoli florets and other vegetables in a sealed, refrigerated container. For stir-fry dishes, heat a little oil in a nonstick pan, toss in the veggies and season with soy sauce, fresh ginger, garlic and a hint of Asian sesame oil. Serve with brown rice.

one pot

rush hour

Caribbean Gingered Squash, Rice and Kale

makes 4 servings

Squash and kale are winter vegetables, so try this recipe when the thermometer drops. Let the fragrant spices of Caribbean cooking transport you to white-sand beaches and azure lagoons!

1 tablespoon + 1 teaspoon vegetable oil

1 onion, chopped

One 2-pound butternut squash, peeled, seeded and cut into 2" chunks

2 jalapeño peppers, seeded, deveined and minced (wear gloves to prevent irritation)

2 teaspoons grated peeled gingerroot

3 garlic cloves, minced

1 teaspoon curry powder

Pinch ground cloves

Pinch ground allspice

1 bunch kale, cleaned and chopped

⅔ cup brown rice

1 teaspoon salt

¼ teaspoon freshly ground black pepper

2 tablespoons fresh lime juice

1. In a large nonstick skillet, heat the oil. Add the onion; cook, stirring as needed, until softened, about 5 minutes. Add the squash, jalapeños, ginger, garlic, curry, cloves and allspice; sauté, stirring, about 1 minute.

2. Add the kale in handfuls, stirring as it wilts. Stir in the rice, salt, pepper and 1½ cups water; bring to a boil. Reduce the heat and simmer until the water is absorbed, 35–40 minutes. Remove from the heat; add the lime juice and fluff with a fork. Let stand, covered, 5 minutes.

serving provides: 1 Bread, 1 Fruit/Vegetable, 1 Fat.

per serving: 251 Calories, 6 g Total Fat, 1 g Saturated Fat, 0 mg Cholesterol, 647 mg Sodium, 45 g Total Carbohydrate, 6 g Dietary Fiber, 6 g Protein, 146 mg Calcium.

POINTS per serving: 4.

one pot

rush hour

(See photo insert.)

Good Advice

In a produce rut? Then try...

1. **Butternut squash.**
   This firm-textured, sweet squash has a melt-in-your-mouth, mellow flavor.

2. **Kale.**
   This winter green is hardy and fresh when the produce aisle is at its most desolate.

3. **Papaya.**
   Smooth and creamy as pudding, sweet with peppery seeds, few fruits satisfy the way a papaya does.

4. **Shiitake, oyster or portobello mushrooms.**
   Once available only in pricey gourmet shops, these earthy treasures are now stocked in supermarkets year-round.

5. **Broccoli rabe.**
   With a rich, slightly bitter taste, broccoli rabe pairs perfectly with garlic and a touch of olive oil to elevate ordinary pasta to a special meal.

6. **Cherimoyas.**
   A South American treat covered in green, armor-like scales, a cherimoya tastes like a cross between a banana and a strawberry. Cut it open and eat the creamy white flesh with a spoon. Remove the large seeds.

7. **Okra.**
   A Southern favorite, this cherished vegetable will add a unique flavor to many recipes.

8. **Clementines.**
   They look like mini, globe-shaped tangerines and they taste like concentrated sunshine.

9. **Mangoes.**
   Luscious and sweet, ripe and fragrant, a mango tastes a little like an apricot, a little like an orange and a lot like heaven.

10. **Star fruit.**
    When cut crosswise, this tangy, sweet citrus fruit makes star-shape slices. Give it a starring role in your next fruit salad or simply award yourself a gold "star" for trying something new.

Fragrant Rice and Black-Eyed Pea Sauté

makes 4 servings

Fresh herbs really wake up black-eyed peas and rice. If you prefer to use fresh, dried or frozen peas, substitute 1½ cups cooked peas for the canned.

2 teaspoons olive oil

1 onion, chopped

4 plum tomatoes, diced

2 cups Perfect Brown Rice (page 12)

One 15-ounce can black-eyed peas, rinsed and drained

3 tablespoons chopped flat-leaf parsley

1 tablespoon chopped basil

2 teaspoons minced rosemary

1 teaspoon minced thyme

2 tablespoons fresh lemon juice

½ teaspoon salt

¼ teaspoon freshly ground black pepper

In a large nonstick skillet, heat the oil. Add the onion; cook, stirring as needed, until softened, about 5 minutes. Add the tomatoes; cook, stirring, 1 minute. Stir in the rice, peas, parsley, basil, rosemary and thyme; cook, tossing gently, until heated through, about 3 minutes. Stir in the lemon juice, salt and pepper.

serving provides: 1 Bread, 1 Fruit/Vegetable, 1 Protein/Milk, 1 Fat.

per serving: 235 Calories, 4 g Total Fat, 1 g Saturated Fat, 0 mg Cholesterol, 515 mg Sodium, 43 g Total Carbohydrate, 5 g Dietary Fiber, 8 g Protein, 65 mg Calcium.

POINTS per serving: 4.

one pot

rush hour

Asian Barley Sauté

makes 4 servings

This sauté has all the great flavoring of Asian cooking, and the barley enhances it perfectly. To save time, make the barley ahead and store it in the refrigerator.

½ cup pearl barley

1 tablespoon vegetable oil

½ pound shiitake mushrooms, diced (about 4 cups)

2 cups trimmed snow peas, diagonally sliced

8 scallions, thinly sliced

1 tablespoon grated peeled gingerroot

Two 8-ounce cans sliced water chestnuts, drained

½ cup orange juice

2 tablespoons reduced-sodium soy sauce

½ teaspoon grated orange zest

1. Cook the barley according to package directions, either in the microwave or conventionally. In a large nonstick skillet, heat the oil. Add the mushrooms; cook, stirring as needed, until golden, 5–6 minutes.

2. Add the barley, snow peas, scallions and ginger; cook, stirring as needed, until the snow peas are softened, 1–2 minutes. Stir in the water chestnuts, orange juice and soy sauce; cook, stirring as needed, until the liquid is absorbed, about 5 minutes. Stir in the orange zest.

serving provides: 1 Bread, 2 Fruit/Vegetables, 1 Fat.

per serving: 244 Calories, 4 g Total Fat, 1 g Saturated Fat, 0 mg Cholesterol, 323 mg Sodium, 49 g Total Carbohydrate, 8 g Dietary Fiber, 6 g Protein, 53 mg Calcium.

POINTS **per serving:** 4.

hint
Use zesty Asian condiments, like chili bean sauce or chili oil, to add heat to recipes; for a spicy flavor, experiment with curry paste; for sweet and spicy, use hoisin sauce. Also lending an Asian flair are tamari, oyster and black-bean sauces.

make ahead

one pot

microwave

spicy

Pipérade

makes 4 servings

Pronounced PEE-pay-rod, this Basque specialty is a divine way to savor the bounty of peppers and tomatoes in the summer; serve it with plenty of crusty bread on the side. Omit the eggs to make a delightful side dish or pasta topping.

1 tablespoon + 1 teaspoon olive oil

6 tomatoes, cut into 1" chunks

3 green bell peppers, seeded and cut into 1" pieces

2 onions, coarsely chopped

1 mild green chile (try Anaheim or Poblano), thinly sliced

2 garlic cloves, minced

1 teaspoon dried oregano

½ teaspoon dried marjoram

Pinch salt

Freshly ground black pepper, to taste

4 eggs, lightly beaten

1. In a medium nonstick skillet, heat 2 teaspoons of the oil. Add the tomatoes; reduce the heat and simmer, stirring as needed, until softened, about 10 minutes (watch for burning).

2. Meanwhile, in a large nonstick skillet, heat the remaining 2 teaspoons of the oil. Add the bell peppers, onions, chile and garlic; cook, stirring as needed, until softened, 15–20 minutes. Stir in the tomatoes, oregano, marjoram, salt and pepper; cook, stirring as needed, until the flavors are blended, about 5 minutes. Pour in the eggs; cook, stirring, until the eggs are set, 2–3 minutes.

serving provides: 3 Fruit/Vegetables, 1 Protein/Milk, 1 Fat.

per serving: 202 Calories, 10 g Total Fat, 2 g Saturated Fat, 212 mg Cholesterol, 83 mg Sodium, 20 g Total Carbohydrate, 4 g Dietary Fiber, 9 g Protein, 65 mg Calcium.

POINTS per serving: 4.

hint
Don't fall into a bland-food trap. Always have barbecue, soy or teriyaki sauce on hand; ditto for spicy extras like salsa, wasabi (Japanese horseradish paste) and a host of sharp, pungent mustards.

Sweet-and-Sour Cabbage
with Peanuts

makes 4 servings

Since this hearty dish relies mostly on pantry staples, it's an easy, delicious fix when your cupboard seems bare. It's perfect over rice or potatoes.

1 onion, chopped

1 small green cabbage, chopped

2 carrots, thinly sliced

½ cup canned crushed tomatoes (no salt added)

¼ cup red-wine vinegar

1 tablespoon sugar

½ teaspoon salt

Freshly ground black pepper, to taste

½ cup unsalted dry-roasted peanuts, chopped

1 cup plain nonfat yogurt

1. Spray a large nonstick skillet with nonstick cooking spray; heat. Add the onion; cook, stirring as needed, until softened, about 5 minutes.

2. Add the cabbage, carrots and ½ cup water; cook, stirring as needed, until the carrots are softened, 5–6 minutes. Stir in the tomatoes, vinegar, sugar, salt and pepper; cook, stirring as needed, until heated through, 2–3 minutes. Sprinkle evenly with the peanuts; serve topped with the yogurt.

serving provides: 2 Fruit/Vegetables, 1 Protein/Milk, 1 Fat.

per serving: 214 Calories, 10 g Total Fat, 1 g Saturated Fat, 1 mg Cholesterol, 374 mg Sodium, 26 g Total Carbohydrate, 6 g Dietary Fiber, 10 g Protein, 202 mg Calcium.

***POINTS* per serving:** 4.

one pot

rush hour

Curried Cauliflower with Black Beans

makes 4 servings

This colorful and flavorful entrée is a great quick fix when you're craving curry but don't have a lot of time. It tastes even better a day later!

1 tablespoon + 1 teaspoon vegetable oil

1 teaspoon curry powder

½ teaspoon ground cumin

½ teaspoon ground coriander

1 small cauliflower, cored and separated into florets

½ teaspoon crushed red pepper flakes

One 14-ounce can crushed tomatoes (no salt added)

One 19-ounce can black beans, rinsed and drained

2 tablespoons minced cilantro

1. In a large nonstick skillet, heat the oil. Add the curry, cumin and coriander; cook, stirring, until just fragrant, 10–15 seconds. Add the cauliflower, pepper flakes and ¼ cup water; cook, stirring as needed, until the cauliflower is well-coated and nearly all of the liquid is evaporated, 3–4 minutes.

2. Add the tomatoes and ¼ cup water; cook, covered, stirring as needed, until slightly thickened, about 10 minutes. Gently stir in the black beans; cook until heated through, 2–3 minutes. Sprinkle with the cilantro.

serving provides: 2 Fruit/Vegetables, 2 Protein/ Milks, 1 Fat.

per serving: 176 Calories, 6 g Total Fat, 1 g Saturated Fat, 0 mg Cholesterol, 274 mg Sodium, 26 g Total Carbohydrate, 10 g Dietary Fiber, 9 g Protein, 82 mg Calcium.

POINTS **per serving:** 2.

make ahead

one pot

rush hour

Pad Thai

makes 4 servings

Everyone loves this delightful stir-fried noodle dish from Thailand. Here, we've eliminated the traditional fish sauce and dried shrimp, replacing them with soy sauce and savory mushrooms.

¼ **pound vermicelli or spaghetti**

10 **dried Chinese black mushroom caps (about 1 ounce)**★

2 **teaspoons vegetable oil**

8 **scallions, minced**

1 **garlic clove, minced**

1 **teaspoon hot chile paste**†

¼ **cup fresh lime juice**

2 **tablespoons reduced–sodium soy sauce**

1 **tablespoon sugar**

3 **egg whites**

1 **cup bean sprouts**

¼ **cup unsalted dry-roasted peanuts, chopped**

Cilantro leaves, to garnish (optional)

1. Cook the vermicelli according to package directions. Drain and keep warm.

2. Meanwhile, in a small saucepan, bring 1 cup water to a boil; add the mushrooms, cover and remove from the heat. Let stand 20 min-utes to soften. Drain, discarding the liquid and squeezing out the excess water. Thinly slice the mushrooms and set aside.

3. In a large nonstick skillet or wok, heat the oil. Add the scallions and garlic; cook, stir-ring as needed, until the scallions are softened, 3–4 minutes. Add the chile paste; cook, stir-ring constantly, until fragrant, about 10 sec-onds. Add the lime juice, soy sauce and sugar; cook, stirring, until the sugar dissolves, about 30 seconds.

4. Add the mushrooms; cook, stirring as needed, until they have absorbed some of the sauce, about 1 minute. Stir in the egg whites; cook, stirring gently, until they begin to set, about 30 seconds. Add the vermicelli and bean sprouts; cook, tossing gently, until mixed and heated through, 2–3 minutes. Serve, sprinkled with the peanuts and cilantro (if using).

serving provides: 2 Breads, 1 Fruit/Vegetable, 1 Fat.

per serving: 246 Calories, 7 g Total Fat, 1 g Saturated Fat, 0 mg Cholesterol, 370 mg Sodium, 41 g Total Carbohydrate, 3 g Dietary Fiber, 7 g Protein, 35 mg Calcium.

POINTS **per serving:** 5.

hint
For an Asian flair, try rice noodles instead of the vermicelli: They need to be soaked in warm water for about 20 minutes, then drained. Add them to soups or other stir-fried dishes as well.

★Made from dried shiitake mushrooms, dried Chi-nese black mushroom caps impart a smoky, meatlike flavor to many dishes. They can be found in Asian markets. If unavailable, substitute ½ cup sliced fresh shiitake mushrooms.

† Made from mashed red hot chile peppers, vin-egar and seasonings (often including garlic), hot chile paste adds fiery zest to many dishes. Stored in the refrigerator, it will keep well over a year, but its potency will decrease as it ages. Find it in Asian markets and gourmet stores; if unavailable, substitute crushed red pepper flakes.

spicy

Sautéed Swiss Chard and Chickpeas

makes 4 servings

Earthy Swiss chard and complex Indian spices makes this dish unbelievably rich and satisfying; serve it with warmed pita bread or brown rice. And don't worry about the small amount of butter; since it's browned, only a bit adds a big flavor punch. If your market has ruby or rhubarb chard, their red stalks will look especially pretty.

hint
Using packaged *garam masala* ("hot spice blend" in Hindu) makes preparation a little simpler; look for it in your local gourmet store or Indian market. If unavailable, blend your own with ½ teaspoon ground cardamom, ¼ teaspoon ground coriander, a pinch of cinnamon and of freshly ground black pepper.

2 teaspoons corn oil

2 teaspoons unsalted butter

½ teaspoon ground cumin

1 tablespoon chopped green chiles (optional)

1 garlic clove, minced

1 bunch Swiss chard, cleaned and chopped (separate the stems and leaves)

One 19-ounce can chickpeas, rinsed and drained

½ teaspoon ground ginger

¾ teaspoon *garam masala*

1. In a large nonstick saucepan, heat the oil and butter, stirring constantly, until the butter melts and the bubbling nearly subsides. Add the cumin; cook, stirring, until just fra-grant, 10–15 seconds. Add the chiles and garlic; cook, stirring constantly, until the garlic is lightly browned, 30–45 seconds.

2. Immediately add the chard stems, the chickpeas and ¼ cup water; cook, stirring gently, until the stems are softened and most of the liquid is evaporated, 3–4 minutes. Stir in the chard leaves, ginger and another ¼ cup water. Reduce the heat and simmer, stirring as needed, until the greens are just tender, 4–5 minutes. Sprinkle with the *garam masala*; cook, uncovered, stirring gently, until the remaining liquid is absorbed, 1–2 minutes.

serving provides: 2 Fruit/Vegetables, 2 Protein/Milks, 1 Fat.

per serving: 166 Calories, 6 g Total Fat, 2 g Saturated Fat, 5 mg Cholesterol, 157 mg Sodium, 20 g Total Carbohydrate, 7 g Dietary Fiber, 8 g Protein, 97 mg Calcium.

POINTS per serving: 2.

one pot

rush hour

chapter five

CASSEROLES
& STEWS

Chickpea and Vegetable Tagine

makes 4 servings

A tagine is a Moroccan stew traditionally simmered in an earthenware pot with a cone-shape lid. We've simplified the technique, using a saucepan, but we've left the exotic aroma and the delicious flavors for you to savor.

1 tablespoon vegetable oil

2 onions, chopped

3 garlic cloves, minced

1½ teaspoons ground cumin

½ teaspoon freshly ground black pepper

¼ teaspoon cinnamon

3 carrots, cut into chunks

One 2-pound butternut squash, peeled, seeded and cut into chunks

One 19-ounce can chickpeas, rinsed and drained

One 14-ounce can diced tomatoes (no salt added)

2 small sweet potatoes, peeled and cut into chunks (about 1 cup)

3 parsnips, peeled and cut into chunks

1 bay leaf

¼ cup chopped flat-leaf parsley

1. In a large saucepan, heat the oil. Add the onions; cook, stirring as needed, until softened, about 5 minutes. Add the garlic; cook, stirring, about 1 minute. Add the cumin, pepper and cinnamon; cook, stirring, 1 minute.

2. Stir in the carrots, squash, chickpeas, tomatoes, sweet potatoes, parsnips, bay leaf and 1 cup water; bring to a boil. Reduce the heat and simmer, partially covered, until the vegetables are tender, 45–55 minutes; discard the bay leaf. Sprinkle with the parsley and serve.

serving provides: 2 Breads, 1 Fruit/Vegetable, 2 Protein/Milks, 1 Fat.

per serving: 380 Calories, 6 g Total Fat, 1 g Saturated Fat, 0 mg Cholesterol, 193 mg Sodium, 74 g Total Carbohydrate, 17 g Dietary Fiber, 12 g Protein, 214 mg Calcium.

POINTS per serving: 5.

make ahead

one pot

Black Bean Chili

makes 4 servings

This recipe is an easy and delicious way to get more soy into your diet. Soybean grits are cracked toasted soybeans, sold in natural food stores.

¼ cup soybean grits

2 teaspoons vegetable oil

1½ onions, diced

1 green bell pepper, seeded and diced

3 carrots, diced

1 medium zucchini, halved length-wise and sliced

1 tablespoon + 1 teaspoon chili powder

3 garlic cloves, minced

½ teaspoon ground cumin

¼ teaspoon cinnamon

Pinch ground cloves

One 28-ounce can whole plum tomatoes (no salt added)

One 15-ounce can black beans, rinsed and drained

2 tablespoons tomato paste (no salt added)

½ teaspoon freshly ground black pepper

½ teaspoon salt

1. In a small saucepan, bring the soybean grits and ¾ cup water to a boil. Reduce the heat and simmer, covered, until the water is absorbed, about 40 minutes.

2. In a large saucepan, heat the oil. Add the onions and bell pepper; cook, stirring as needed, until softened, about 5 minutes. Add the carrots, zucchini, chili powder, garlic, cumin, cinnamon and cloves; cook, stirring, about 1 minute. Stir in the tomatoes, black beans, tomato paste, pepper, salt and soybean grits. Cook, covered, stirring as needed, until thickened, about 1 hour.

serving provides: 3 Fruit/Vegetables, 2 Protein/Milks, 1 Fat.

per serving: 232 Calories, 5 g Total Fat, 1 g Saturated Fat, 0 mg Cholesterol, 547 mg Sodium, 39 g Total Carbohydrate, 14 g Dietary Fiber, 12 g Protein, 143 mg Calcium.

POINTS **per serving:** 2.

hint

Instant dinner: Sauté green bell peppers, garlic and onion, then stir in drained rinsed canned black beans and seasoned stewed tomatoes; serve over brown rice.

make ahead

spicy

Indian Lentil and Vegetable Stew

makes 4 servings

Indian lentils are yellow. If you have an international food store nearby, look for them under the name toovar dal. *Yellow split peas make a fine substitute. If you're sensitive to hot and spicy foods, by all means seed and devein the chile—although including the seeds and veins gives a more authentic flavor.*

½ cup yellow lentils or split peas, picked over, rinsed and drained

½ teaspoon turmeric

1 tablespoon + 1 teaspoon vegetable oil

2 teaspoons mustard seeds

3 garlic cloves, minced

1 serrano chile, thinly sliced (wear gloves to prevent irritation)

One 10-ounce package frozen Brussels sprouts, thawed

1 cup canned diced tomatoes (no salt added)

½ teaspoon salt

1 tablespoon fresh lemon juice

1 tablespoon chopped cilantro

1. In a medium saucepan, combine the lentils, turmeric and 1 cup water; bring to a boil. Reduce the heat and simmer until the lentils are soft, about 30 minutes. Transfer to a blender or food processor and puree.

2. In a large nonstick skillet, heat the oil. Add the mustard seeds; cook, covered, until the popping subsides, 1–2 minutes. Add the garlic and chile; cook, stirring, about 1 minute. Stir in the Brussels sprouts, tomatoes, salt and ¾ cup water; cook, covered, until the Brussels sprouts are tender, about 10 minutes. Stir in the pureed lentils; cook until heated through, about 5 minutes. Remove from the heat and stir in the lemon juice and cilantro.

serving provides: 1 Fruit/Vegetable, 1 Protein/Milk, 1 Fat.

per serving: 205 Calories, 6 g Total Fat, 1 g Saturated Fat, 0 mg Cholesterol, 350 mg Sodium, 31 g Total Carbohydrate, 6 g Dietary Fiber, 10 g Protein, 107 mg Calcium.

POINTS per serving: 3.

make ahead

spicy

Cannellini Bean and Escarole Stew

makes 4 servings

Serve this fast, flavorful, Italian-inspired dish over steaming rice for a satisfying meal. The escarole will wilt quite a bit, so don't worry about chopping it too fine—2" pieces are about right.

2 teaspoons olive oil

2 onions, chopped

1 bunch escarole, cleaned and coarsely chopped

3 garlic cloves, minced

½ teaspoon salt

½ teaspoon freshly ground black pepper

One 15–ounce can cannellini beans, rinsed and drained

One 14–ounce can diced tomatoes (no salt added)

In a medium nonstick skillet, heat the oil. Add the onions; cook, stirring as needed, until softened, about 5 minutes. Add the escarole, garlic, salt and pepper; cook, stirring as needed, until the escarole is wilted, about 3 minutes. Stir in the beans and tomatoes; simmer, covered, until the flavors are blended, about 10 minutes.

serving provides: 2 Fruit/Vegetables, 1 Protein/ Milk, 1 Fat.

per serving: 142 Calories, 3 g Total Fat, 0 g Saturated Fat, 0 mg Cholesterol, 490 mg Sodium, 24 g Total Carbohydrate, 7 g Dietary Fiber, 7 g Protein, 104 mg Calcium.

POINTS **per serving:** 2.

hint

Escarole (broad-leaf endive), a green related to chicory but not nearly as bitter, is flavorful in salads, lightly sautéed or eaten raw. In Italy, it's a popular ingredient in soups and stews.

one pot

rush hour

Turkish White Bean Stew

makes 4 servings

A variation on this stew can be found in just about every home kitchen and restaurant in Turkey. It is so simple and satisfying, it's worth adopting on this side of the Atlantic.

1 cup great Northern beans, picked over, rinsed and drained

2 teaspoons olive oil

2 onions, chopped

2 carrots, chopped

2 celery stalks, chopped

3 garlic cloves, minced

¼ cup tomato paste (no salt added)

1 teaspoon sugar

Pinch crushed red pepper flakes

2 tablespoons chopped flat-leaf parsley

2 tablespoons fresh lemon juice

½ teaspoon salt

1. Soak the beans (see page 6).

2. In a medium saucepan, bring the beans and 3 cups water to a boil. Reduce the heat and simmer, partially covered, 30 minutes. Drain, leaving the beans in the saucepan.

3. In a medium nonstick skillet, heat the oil. Add the onions; cook, stirring as needed, until softened, about 5 minutes. Add the carrots, celery and garlic; cook, stirring as needed, until the celery is golden, about 5 minutes.

4. In the saucepan, combine the beans with the onion mixture. Add the tomato paste, sugar, pepper flakes and 2 cups water; bring to a boil. Reduce the heat and simmer, covered, until the beans are tender, about 1 hour. Add half of the parsley, the lemon juice and salt; cook 10 minutes. Serve, sprinkled with the remaining parsley.

serving provides: 1 Fruit/Vegetable, 2 Protein/ Milks, 1 Fat.

per serving: 255 Calories, 3 g Total Fat, 0 g Saturated Fat, 0 mg Cholesterol, 54 mg Sodium, 46 g Total Carbohydrate, 11 g Dietary Fiber, 14 g Protein, 169 mg Calcium.

POINTS **per serving:** 3.

make ahead

Wheat Berry–Vegetable Stew

makes 4 servings

Wheat berries are whole kernels of wheat; their flavor is slightly sweet, slightly nutty and utterly delicious. Find them in natural food stores.

½ cup wheat berries

2 teaspoons olive oil

1 onion, sliced

2 garlic cloves, minced

2 cups cauliflower florets

1 medium zucchini, halved lengthwise and sliced

1 medium yellow squash, halved lengthwise and sliced

1 cup canned diced tomatoes (no salt added)

1 teaspoon minced rosemary

¼ teaspoon freshly ground black pepper

¼ teaspoon salt

¼ cup chopped basil

¼ cup chopped flat-leaf parsley

½ teaspoon minced thyme

1. In a medium saucepan, combine the wheat berries and 2 cups water; bring to a boil. Reduce the heat and simmer, covered, until softened but not tender, about 1 hour. (To prepare in a microwave, combine the wheat berries and 2 cups water in a microwavable dish. With a vented cover, microwave on High until the water comes to a boil, 7 minutes; microwave at 40% power, 50 minutes.)

2. In a medium nonstick skillet, heat the oil. Add the onion; cook, stirring as needed, until softened, about 5 minutes. Add the garlic; cook, stirring, about 1 minute. Stir in the wheat berries, cauliflower, zucchini, squash, tomatoes, rosemary, pepper, salt and 1 cup water; bring to a boil. Reduce the heat and simmer until the wheat berries and vegetables are tender, about 30 minutes. Stir in the basil, parsley and thyme.

serving provides: 1 Bread, 2 Fruit/Vegetables, 1 Fat.

per serving: 169 Calories, 3 g Total Fat, 0 g Saturated Fat, 0 mg Cholesterol, 176 mg Sodium, 31 g Total Carbohydrate, 4 g Dietary Fiber, 6 g Protein, 67 mg Calcium.
POINTS per serving: 3.

hint
Look for simple ways to pile on the veggies. Add extra carrots to soups; spinach to lasagna; a handful of pepper strips to a stir-fried dish; or peas to a casserole.

make ahead

microwave

(See photo insert.)

Japanese Winter Vegetable Stew with Miso

makes 4 servings

This is a real home-style Japanese stew. Daikon, also called Japanese white radish, has the sharp taste and crisp texture of radish, but it can grow to be more than one foot long. Look for it at Asian markets. Mirin is a sweet rice wine common in Japanese kitchens; if it's unavailable, substitute sweet sherry.

2 teaspoons vegetable oil

1 pound Pressed Tofu (page 8), cubed

2 large all-purpose potatoes, peeled and cubed

2 carrots, cubed

1 cup sliced daikon radish

1 onion, diced

½ cup mirin

¼ cup miso

1 tablespoon sugar

1. In a large nonstick skillet, heat the oil. Add the tofu; cook, stirring as needed, until golden, 5–6 minutes. Add 2 cups water; bring to a boil. Stir in the potatoes, carrots, daikon and onion; return to a boil. Reduce the heat and simmer until the potatoes are tender, about 20 minutes.

2. In a small bowl, combine the mirin, miso, sugar and ¼ cup of the vegetable cooking liquid. Stir into the vegetable mixture.

serving provides: 1 Bread, 1 Fruit/Vegetable, 2 Protein/Milks, 80 Bonus Calories.

per serving: 301 Calories, 6 g Total Fat, 0 g Saturated Fat, 0 mg Cholesterol, 658 mg Sodium, 41 g Total Carbohydrate, 7 g Dietary Fiber, 17 g Protein, 95 mg Calcium.

POINTS per serving: 5.

make ahead

Greek Potato-Zucchini Casserole

makes 6 servings

This simple vegetable casserole is a typical dish in many Greek tavernas.

One 14-ounce can diced tomatoes (no salt added)

¼ cup minced dill

2 tablespoons chopped flat-leaf parsley

2 garlic cloves, minced

½ teaspoon salt

¼ teaspoon freshly ground black pepper

4 small all-purpose potatoes, peeled and sliced

2 medium zucchini, sliced lengthwise

2 green bell peppers, seeded and sliced

2 onions, sliced

1 cup crumbled feta cheese

1. Preheat the oven to 350° F. Spray a shallow 2-quart casserole with nonstick cooking spray. In a small bowl, combine the tomatoes, dill, parsley, garlic, salt and pepper. In the casserole, layer half of the potatoes, zucchini, bell peppers, onions and the tomato mixture; repeat the layers.

2. Bake, covered with foil, until the vegetables are cooked through and soft, 1¼–1½ hours. Sprinkle with the cheese; bake, uncovered, until the cheese is melted, about 15 minutes. Cover loosely with foil and let stand 10 minutes before serving.

serving provides: 1 Bread, 1 Fruit/Vegetable, 1 Protein/Milk.

per serving: 230 Calories, 9 g Total Fat, 6 g Saturated Fat, 38 mg Cholesterol, 684 mg Sodium, 29 g Total Carbohydrate, 4 g Dietary Fiber, 9 g Protein, 256 mg Calcium.

POINTS **per serving:** 5.

hint

When eating out, ask for salad dressing on the side. Instead of pouring it on the salad, dip the tines of your fork in the dressing before stabbing into a forkful of greens.

one pot

Baked Barley with Mushrooms

makes 4 servings

With the earthy flavor of mushrooms and the intense, slightly sweet flavor of sun-dried tomatoes, this hearty dish will become a family favorite. It also makes a wonderful side dish.

hint
Choose
oil carefully.
Sesame, hazelnut
or porcini-
mushroom olive
oil packs lots of
flavor with the
same calories as
does vegetable
oil. While they're
too delicate for
sautéing, the
stronger flavor
means you'll need
less in salads.

8 sun-dried tomato halves (not oil-packed)

2 teaspoons olive oil

2 carrots, finely diced

2 shallots, minced

2 portobello mushrooms, diced

½ teaspoon thyme leaves

1¾ cups Vegetable Broth (page 2)

1 cup pearl barley

½ teaspoon salt

¼ teaspoon freshly ground black pepper

¾ cup grated part-skim mozzarella cheese

1. Preheat the oven to 350° F. In a small bowl, soak the tomatoes in warm water until pliable, about 10 minutes. In a medium nonstick skillet, heat the oil. Add the carrots and shallots; cook, stirring as needed, until softened, 4–5 minutes. Stir in the mushrooms and thyme; cook, stirring as needed, until wilted, 7–8 minutes.

2. Transfer the mixture to an 8"-square baking dish. Stir in the broth, barley, tomatoes, salt and pepper. Bake, covered with foil, until the liquid is absorbed, about 1 hour. Sprinkle with cheese and bake, uncovered, until the cheese is melted, about 10 minutes.

serving provides: 2 Breads, 2 Fruit/Vegetables, 1 Protein/Milk, 1 Fat.

per serving: 302 Calories, 6 g Total Fat, 3 g Saturated Fat, 12 mg Cholesterol, 515 mg Sodium, 50 g Total Carbohydrate, 9 g Dietary Fiber, 13 g Protein, 168 mg Calcium.

POINTS per serving: 5.

Summer Harvest Stew

makes 4 servings

In late July, these ingredients are at their peak at farmers' markets. This dish cooks just briefly, so the flavors stay fresh and true.

1 tablespoon + 1 teaspoon extra virgin olive oil

2 onions, coarsely chopped

2 garlic cloves, minced

2 tomatoes, coarsely chopped

2 cups fresh or thawed frozen okra, cut in ½" pieces

2 cups fresh or thawed frozen corn kernels

1 cup Vegetable Broth (page 2)

¼ teaspoon salt

¼ teaspoon freshly ground black pepper

2 tablespoons chopped basil

1. In a large nonstick skillet, heat the oil. Add the onions; cook, stirring as needed, until softened, about 5 minutes. Add the garlic; cook, stirring, about 1 minute.

2. Stir in the tomatoes, okra, corn, broth, salt and pepper; bring to a boil. Reduce the heat and simmer, stirring as needed, until the okra is softened, about 5 minutes. Stir in the basil.

serving provides: 1 Bread, 1 Fruit/Vegetable, 1 Fat.

per serving: 164 Calories, 5 g Total Fat, 1 g Saturated Fat, 0 mg Cholesterol, 221 mg Sodium, 27 g Total Carbohydrate, 5 g Dietary Fiber, 5 g Protein, 54 mg Calcium.

POINTS per serving: 3.

one pot

rush hour

(See photo insert.)

Mexican Casserole

makes 4 servings

Substitute any cooked beans for the cranberry beans; black beans provide a beautiful color contrast.

2 teaspoons vegetable oil

1 carrot, diced

1 onion, chopped

One 1-pound butternut squash, peeled, seeded and cubed

1 tablespoon chili powder

2 teaspoons ground cumin

2 garlic cloves, minced

One 19-ounce can cranberry beans, rinsed and drained

One 14-ounce can whole tomatoes (no salt added)

1 teaspoon dried oregano

¼ teaspoon ground cloves

¼ teaspoon cayenne pepper

¾ teaspoon salt

½ cup yellow cornmeal

⅓ cup shredded Monterey Jack cheese

½ red bell pepper, seeded and finely diced

2 tablespoons chopped cilantro

½ teaspoon freshly ground black pepper

1. In a medium nonstick skillet, heat the oil. Add the carrot and onion; cook, stirring as needed, until softened, about 5 minutes. Add the squash, chili powder, cumin and garlic; cook, stirring as needed, until the onion is golden, 4–5 minutes longer. Stir in the beans, tomatoes, oregano, cloves, cayenne and ¼ teaspoon of the salt; bring to a boil. Reduce the heat and simmer, breaking up the tomatoes with a spoon and stirring as needed, until thickened, 18–20 minutes.

2. Meanwhile, preheat the oven to 350°F. In a medium saucepan, combine the cornmeal, the remaining ½ teaspoon of salt and 2 cups water; bring to a boil, whisking constantly. Reduce the heat and simmer, whisking constantly, until the mixture is very thick and pulls away from the sides of the pan, about 15 minutes. Cool slightly, then stir in the cheese, bell pepper, cilantro and black pepper.

3. Transfer the squash mixture to a 9"-square baking dish; top with the cornmeal mixture. Bake until the casserole is bubbling and lightly browned, about 40 minutes.

serving provides: 2 Breads, 1 Fruit/Vegetable, 2 Protein/Milks, 1 Fat.

per serving: 339 Calories, 7 g Total Fat, 2 g Saturated Fat, 10 mg Cholesterol, 932 mg Sodium, 61 g Total Carbohydrate, 12 g Dietary Fiber, 13 g Protein, 236 mg Calcium.

***POINTS* per serving:** 5.

make ahead

(See photo insert.)

veggie tortilla roll-ups

summer harvest stew

white bean risotto with fragrant herbs

veggie paella

wheat berry–vegetable stew

fettuccine with creamy spinach sauce

caribbean gingered squash, rice and kale

spinach pie

pear, walnut and feta salad

super stacked salad sandwiches and spicy baked sweet potato chips

mexican casserole

indian tomato-lentil soup

spicy chickpea samosas and "stuffed" cherry tomatoes

creamy spinach and pepper lasagna

rigatoni with "meat" sauce

carmelized onion and tomato calzone

Good Advice

To get the most out of the protein you are consuming:

1. Include a variety of legumes, dairy products, whole grains and dark leafy greens to compensate for lacking B vitamins from not eating meat.

2. Pair black, pinto and cannellini beans with vegetables high in vitamin C, like tomatoes and red peppers—the vitamin boosts the body's ability to absorb the iron from the beans.

3. Don't rely on dairy products as your primary protein source. Although cheese provides calcium as well as protein, unless it's labeled reduced-fat or nonfat, it contributes excessive amounts of fat and calories to your diet. Better sources of protein include legumes, grains, vegetables and reduced-fat dairy foods.

4. Use Textured Vegetable Protein crumbles (now available in the frozen-foods section of supermarkets) as a meat substitute. Their texture is remarkably like ground beef, and so they work wonderfully in tacos, chili and sloppy joe recipes. Just cook as you would regular ground beef.

Shepherd's Garden Pie

Tofu replaces the traditional lamb in this new vegetarian classic. If you like, substitute cauliflower for all or part of the broccoli.

1 tablespoon + 1 teaspoon olive oil

2 onions, chopped

2 cups chopped mushrooms

3 garlic cloves, minced

¼ teaspoon salt

¼ teaspoon freshly ground black pepper

½ pound Frozen Tofu (page 9), crumbled

6 plum tomatoes, diced

4 cups chopped broccoli, cauliflower or combination, steamed

½ cup Vegetable Broth (page 2)

¼ cup chopped flat-leaf parsley

4 large all–purpose potatoes, cooked, peeled and mashed

2 ounces low-fat cream cheese

1. Preheat the oven to 375° F. In a large non-stick skillet, heat the oil. Add the onions; cook, stirring as needed, until softened, about 5 minutes. Add the mushrooms, garlic, salt and pepper; cook, stirring as needed, until the mushrooms are wilted, 8–10 minutes. Stir in the tofu and tomatoes; cook about 3 minutes. Stir in the broccoli, broth and parsley. Transfer to a 9" -square baking dish.

2. In a medium bowl, combine the potatoes and the cream cheese. Spread it over the tofu mixture. Bake until golden, about 30 minutes.

serving provides: 2 Breads, 3 Fruit/Vegetables, 1 Protein/Milk, 1 Fat.

per serving: 456 Calories, 13 g Total Fat, 4 g Saturated Fat, 13 mg Cholesterol, 362 mg Sodium, 70 g Total Carbohydrate, 13 g Dietary Fiber, 21 g Protein, 177 mg Calcium.

POINTS **per serving:** 8.

make ahead

Leek and Egg Casserole

makes 6 servings

Basically a quiche without a crust, this casserole has flavors that are simple yet delicious. Make sure you clean your leeks carefully; sand has a tendency to hide in the layers of leek.

2 teaspoons olive oil

6 leeks, cleaned, halved lengthwise and sliced

¼ cup grated Parmesan cheese

1 cup fat-free egg substitute

1 cup part-skim ricotta cheese

½ cup low-fat (1%) milk

1 teaspoon Dijon mustard

½ teaspoon freshly ground black pepper

½ teaspoon salt

¼ teaspoon grated nutmeg

1. Preheat the oven to 350° F. Spray a pie plate with nonstick cooking spray. In a large nonstick skillet, heat the oil. Add the leeks and 3 tablespoons water; cook, covered, until tender, 12–15 minutes. Uncover and cook until the water is evaporated, about 3 minutes longer. Place the leeks in the pie plate and sprinkle with the Parmesan.

2. In a medium bowl, combine the egg substitute, ricotta, milk, mustard, pepper, salt and nutmeg; pour over the leeks. Bake until the top is golden and puffed and the egg mixture is set, 35–40 minutes. Cool slightly before cutting into 6 wedges.

serving provides: 2 Fruit/Vegetables, 1 Protein/Milk.

per serving: 191 Calories, 6 g Total Fat, 3 g Saturated Fat, 16 mg Cholesterol, 414 mg Sodium, 22 g Total Carbohydrate, 2 g Dietary Fiber, 13 g Protein, 271 mg Calcium.

POINTS per serving: 4.

hint
Be daring with salad greens: Try purslane, a reddish stem and fleshy leaf lettuce with a mild flavor and almost creamy texture. This Greek favorite also contains omega-3 fatty acids (the "heart-healthy" oils found primarily in fish).

Vegetable-Bean Gratin

Throw together this easy casserole for a Sunday supper—it's perfect for late fall or early spring.

2 red bell peppers, seeded and slivered

4 plum tomatoes, diced

2 red onions, slivered

2 celery stalks, thinly sliced

1 tablespoon olive oil

4 garlic cloves, slivered

1 teaspoon minced thyme

One 19–ounce can red kidney beans, rinsed and drained

¼ cup grated Parmesan cheese

Preheat the oven to 400° F. In a shallow 1½-quart baking dish, combine the peppers, tomatoes, onions, celery, oil, garlic and thyme; stir in the beans. Bake, stirring 2–3 times, until the vegetables are tender, about 1 hour. Sprinkle with the cheese; bake until the cheese is melted, about 10 minutes longer.

serving provides: 2 Fruit/Vegetables, 2 Protein/Milks, 1 Fat.

per serving: 249 Calories, 6 g Total Fat, 2 g Saturated Fat, 4 mg Cholesterol, 366 mg Sodium, 40 g Total Carbohydrate, 12 g Dietary Fiber, 12 g Protein, 154 mg Calcium.

POINTS per serving: 3.

make ahead

one pot

Sweet Potato Gratin

makes 4 servings

This sweet treat will please the whole family. Orange and rosemary combine to give this dish an extraordinary flavor.

4 small sweet potatoes, peeled and sliced (about 2 cups)

One 19-ounce can cannellini beans, rinsed and drained

1½ cups orange juice

2 teaspoons olive oil

1 teaspoon minced rosemary

1 garlic clove, minced

½ teaspoon salt

¼ teaspoon freshly ground black pepper

⅓ cup shredded Monterey Jack cheese

Preheat the oven to 375° F. In a 9"-square baking dish, combine the potatoes, beans, orange juice, oil, rosemary, garlic, salt and pepper. Bake, covered, until potatoes are tender, about 45 minutes. Uncover and bake until very little liquid remains, about 30 minutes longer. Sprinkle with the cheese; bake until the cheese is melted, about 10 minutes. Let stand 5 minutes before serving.

serving provides: 1 Bread, 1 Fruit/Vegetable, 2 Protein/Milks, 1 Fat.

per serving: 275 Calories, 6 g Total Fat, 2 g Saturated Fat, 10 mg Cholesterol, 598 mg Sodium, 48 g Total Carbohydrate, 9 g Dietary Fiber, 10 g Protein, 131 mg Calcium.

POINTS **per serving:** 4.

one pot

chapter six

MAIN-COURSE SALADS & SANDWICHES

Mexican Rice and Bean Salad

This salad is sure to be a crowd pleaser. Its colors are so festive and the taste is magnifico.

2 cups Perfect Brown Rice (page 12)

One 19-ounce can black beans, rinsed and drained

3 plum tomatoes, diced

½ cup cooked corn kernels

1 red onion, finely chopped

1 jalapeño pepper, seeded, deveined and minced (wear gloves to prevent irritation)

1 teaspoon coarsely chopped cilantro

1½ teaspoons ground cumin

2 tablespoons fresh lime juice

½ teaspoon salt

¼ teaspoon freshly ground black pepper

1 tablespoon + 1 teaspoon vegetable oil

1. In a large bowl, combine the rice, beans, tomatoes, corn, onion, jalapeño and cilantro.

2. In a small skillet over low heat, heat the cumin until just fragrant, about 1 minute. Transfer to a small bowl; stir in the lime juice, salt and pepper. Whisk in the oil. Pour over the rice mixture; toss to coat.

serving provides: 1 Bread, 2 Protein/Milks, 1 Fat.

per serving: 283 Calories, 6 g Total Fat, 1 g Saturated Fat, 0 mg Cholesterol, 558 mg Sodium, 49 g Total Carbohydrate, 10 g Dietary Fiber, 10 g Protein, 60 mg Calcium.

POINTS per serving: 4.

make ahead

one pot

spicy

Thai Salad with Tofu

makes 4 servings

This sweet-and-spicy salad makes a refreshing summer supper. If you prefer really spicy, go with the higher amount of pepper flakes.

1 tablespoon + 1 teaspoon vegetable oil

1 pound Pressed Tofu (page 8), cubed

4 teaspoons fresh lime juice

1 tablespoon reduced-sodium soy sauce

2 teaspoons sugar

2 garlic cloves, minced

¼–½ teaspoon crushed red pepper flakes

4 cups shredded green leaf, romaine or Boston lettuce

2 cucumbers, peeled, seeded and very thinly sliced

1 sweet onion, slivered

¼ cup whole mint leaves

1. In a large nonstick skillet, heat 2 teaspoons of the oil. Add the tofu; cook, stirring as needed, until golden, 5–6 minutes.

2. In a medium bowl, whisk the remaining 2 teaspoons of oil, the lime juice, soy sauce, sugar, garlic and pepper flakes. Add the tofu, lettuce, cucumber, onion and mint; toss to combine.

serving provides: 2 Fruit/Vegetables, 2 Protein/Milks, 1 Fat.

per serving: 207 Calories, 10 g Total Fat, 1 g Saturated Fat, 0 mg Cholesterol, 170 mg Sodium, 17 g Total Carbohydrate, 5 g Dietary Fiber, 15 g Protein, 132 mg Calcium.

POINTS per serving: 4.

hint
Chill on iceberg lettuce. Darker, leafy greens such as romaine or red leaf have more flavor and more nutrients. Try Butterleaf or Boston varieties for a truly buttery taste and velvety texture.

spicy

Marinated Grilled Vegetable Salad

makes 4 servings

Farm-fresh produce combines to make a savory, hearty salad that only gets better over time. Make it a day ahead when you are grilling—the next day you'll have an instant meal.

hint

Consider
nonmeat
barbecues:
Marinate
eggplant,
zucchini and
portobello
mushrooms in fat-
free Italian
dressing; then
grill them with
soy-based hot
dogs and burgers
for a fast,
flavorful dinner.

1 baby (about ½ pound) eggplant, halved

¾ teaspoon salt

1 fennel bulb, halved

1 medium zucchini, halved

1 red bell pepper, halved and seeded

1 tablespoon + 1 teaspoon extra virgin olive oil

1 red onion, thinly sliced

2 tablespoons balsamic vinegar

2 garlic cloves, crushed

¼ teaspoon freshly ground black pepper

¼ teaspoon minced thyme

1. Spray the broiler or grill rack with non-stick cooking spray; set aside. Preheat the broiler or prepare the grill. Place the eggplant on paper towels and sprinkle with ¼ teaspoon of the salt. Cover with a plate and press 20 minutes. Rinse and squeeze dry between more paper towels.

2. Brush the fennel, zucchini, bell pepper and eggplant with 1 tablespoon of the oil. Broil or grill the vegetables until just cooked through, 6–7 minutes on each side.

3. Cut the vegetables into 1" slices; transfer to a medium bowl. Add the onion, vinegar, garlic, black pepper, thyme, the remaining 1 teaspoon of oil and the remaining ½ teaspoon of salt; toss to combine. Let stand at room temperature until the flavors are blended, at least 3 hours, or refrigerate, covered, overnight.

serving provides: 2 Fruit/Vegetables, 1 Fat.

per serving: 94 Calories, 5 g Total Fat, 1 g Saturated Fat, 0 mg Cholesterol, 308 mg Sodium, 12 g Total Carbohydrate, 3 g Dietary Fiber, 2 g Protein, 28 mg Calcium.

POINTS per serving: 2.

make ahead

Crunchy Apple Salad with Tofu-Dill Dressing

makes 4 servings

In this super-healthful version of Waldorf salad, we've replaced the traditional high-fat mayonnaise with protein-rich Tofu Salad Dressing. If your supermarket has mesclun, the salad-ready blend of gourmet lettuces, use that.

½ cup Tofu Salad Dressing (page 5)

¼ cup minced dill

1 tablespoon fresh lemon juice

2 Granny Smith apples, peeled, cored and thinly sliced

4 celery stalks, thinly sliced

1 red onion, thinly sliced

6 cups shredded mixed salad greens or mesclun

¼ cup walnuts, chopped and toasted*

In a salad bowl, combine the dressing, dill and lemon juice. Add the apples, celery and onion; toss to coat. Serve on beds of greens and sprinkle with the walnuts.

serving provides: 1 Fruit/Vegetable, 1 Protein/Milk, 1 Fat.

per serving: 146 Calories, 8 g Total Fat, 1 g Saturated Fat, 0 mg Cholesterol, 203 mg Sodium, 17 g Total Carbohydrate, 3 g Dietary Fiber, 5 g Protein, 46 mg Calcium.

POINTS per serving: 3.

hint
Next time you see mâche, also known as corn salad, in your produce aisle, try it. This delicate, sweet green with rounded leaves is popular in France and Italy and is often included in the baby salad green mix known as mesclun.

rush hour

★ To toast the walnuts, place them in a small skillet over medium-low heat; cook, shaking the pan and stirring constantly, until lightly browned, 3–5 minutes.

Greek Salad

makes 4 servings

This is typical of the salad available all over Greece. They, of course, don't call it "Greek Salad," but horiatiki, or "village salad." Use fat-free feta cheese if you find it at your supermarket; you'll cut total fat grams to 4, saturated fat grams to 1 in this recipe.

1 tablespoon + 1 teaspoon red-wine vinegar1 tablespoon olive oil

1½ teaspoons minced thyme

¼ teaspoon salt

¼ teaspoon freshly ground black pepper

4 cups sliced romaine lettuce

½ green bell pepper, seeded and diced

½ red bell pepper, seeded and diced

1 tomato, diced

¼ cup minced dill

10 small kalamata olives, pitted and chopped

4 scallions, sliced

1 cup crumbled feta cheese (preferably fat-free)

In a salad bowl, combine the vinegar, oil, thyme, salt and pepper. Add the lettuce, bell pepper, tomato, dill, olives and scallions; toss to coat. Add the cheese; toss gently. Serve at once.

serving provides: 2 Fruit/Vegetables, 1 Protein/Milk, 1 Fat.

per serving: 234 Calories, 18 g Total Fat, 10 g Saturated Fat, 57 mg Cholesterol, 932 mg Sodium, 9 g Total Carbohydrate, 3 g Dietary Fiber, 11 g Protein, 352 mg Calcium.

POINTS per serving: 6.

rush hour

Chickpea, Spelt and Beet Salad

makes 4 servings

Spelt is an ancient grain related to wheat, but it's much richer in nutrients. It has a wonderful nutty flavor. Find it in your natural food store.

½ **cup spelt**

2 large beets, trimmed, cooked, peeled and cubed

1 cup drained rinsed canned chickpeas

¼ **red onion, diced**

¼ **cup plain nonfat yogurt**

2 tablespoons chopped basil

1 tablespoon + 1 teaspoon fresh lemon juice

¼ **teaspoon salt**

¼ **teaspoon freshly ground black pepper**

¼ **cup walnuts, chopped and toasted★**

1. In a small saucepan, combine the spelt and 1½ cups water; bring to a boil. Reduce the heat and simmer until the spelt is tender and the water is absorbed, about 1 hour. Cool to room temperature.

2. In a salad bowl, combine the spelt, beets, chickpeas, onion, yogurt, basil, lemon juice, salt and pepper. Sprinkle with the walnuts.

serving provides: 1 Bread, 1 Fruit/Vegetable, 1 Protein/Milk, 1 Fat.

per serving: 212 Calories, 6 g Total Fat, 0 g Saturated Fat, 0 mg Cholesterol, 255 mg Sodium, 35 g Total Carbohydrate, 8 g Dietary Fiber, 10 g Protein, 63 mg Calcium.

POINTS per serving: 3.

hint

Play up color in your salad: Throw in red and yellow pepper slices, tomato, beets, chopped red onion and creamy mushroom slices for an eye-popping display.

make ahead

one pot

★ To toast the walnuts, place them in a small skillet over medium-low heat; cook, shaking the pan and stirring constantly, until lightly browned, 3–5 minutes.

Fennel-Orange Salad with Garlic Tofu

makes 4 servings

This salad is a great combination of flavors and textures. The greens are bitter, the oranges tangy and juicy, and the tofu is smooth and garlicky.

5 teaspoons extra virgin olive oil

3 garlic cloves, minced

½ pound Pressed Tofu (page 8), cubed

3 tablespoons orange juice

1 teaspoon red-wine vinegar

¼ teaspoon dry mustard

¼ teaspoon salt

¼ teaspoon freshly ground black pepper

1 bunch arugula, cleaned

4 oranges, peeled and sectioned

2 fennel bulbs, thinly sliced

1 red onion, thinly sliced

1 cup basil leaves

1. In a large nonstick skillet, heat 2 teaspoons of the oil. Add the garlic; cook, stirring, about 1 minute. Add the tofu; cook, stirring as needed, until golden, 5–6 minutes.

2. In a medium bowl, combine the orange juice, vinegar, mustard, salt, pepper and the remaining 1 tablespoon of oil. Add the arugula, oranges, fennel, onion and basil; toss to coat. Add the tofu; toss to combine.

serving provides: 3 Fruit/Vegetables, 1 Protein/Milk, 1 Fat.

per serving: 228 Calories, 9 g Total Fat, 1 g Saturated Fat, 0 mg Cholesterol, 350 mg Sodium, 31g Total Carbohydrate, 9 g Dietary Fiber, 10 g Protein, 210 mg Calcium.

POINTS **per serving:** 4.

rush hour

Potato and Egg Salad

makes 4 servings

We've replaced the mayonnaise in everyone's favorite salad with yogurt for a lighter, slightly tangy taste.

¾ cup plain nonfat yogurt

½ sweet onion, minced

1 tablespoon white-wine vinegar

1 tablespoon olive oil

½ teaspoon salt

¼ teaspoon freshly ground black pepper

1 pound new potatoes, cooked and cubed

4 eggs, hard-cooked and quartered

4 celery stalks, chopped

1 green bell pepper, seeded and chopped

2 tablespoons chopped basil

In a large bowl, combine the yogurt, onion, vinegar, oil, salt and pepper. Add the potatoes, eggs, celery, bell pepper and basil; toss to coat. Serve at once or refrigerate, covered, until ready to serve.

serving provides: 1 Bread, 1 Fruit/Vegetable, 1 Protein/Milk, 1 Fat.

per serving: 273 Calories, 9 g Total Fat, 2 g Saturated Fat, 213 mg Cholesterol, 430 mg Sodium, 37 g Total Carbohydrate, 4 g Dietary Fiber, 12 g Protein, 146 mg Calcium.

POINTS **per serving:** 5.

hint
Make potato salad or coleslaw with reduced-calorie mayonnaise or plain nonfat yogurt and mustard, instead of regular mayo.

make ahead

rush hour

Pasta Salad with Yogurt Vinaigrette

makes 4 servings

This salad, with its tangy, creamy dressing, is delicious. Vary the vegetables to suit your preferences and the seasons, and experiment with pastas of different shapes and flavors.

hint

At the salad bar, shun any vegetables marinated in oily dressings. Rather, opt for veggies (including salads) that are raw or steamed—and undressed. At home, add your own dressing sparingly.

½ **cup plain nonfat yogurt**

1 **tablespoon red-wine vinegar**

2 **teaspoons extra virgin olive oil**

½ **teaspoon salt**

¼ **teaspoon freshly ground black pepper**

2½ **cups chopped broccoli, steamed**

2 **cups cooked penne**

2 **carrots, sliced**

1 **red onion, thinly sliced**

In a large bowl, combine the yogurt, vinegar, oil, salt and pepper. Add the broccoli, penne, carrots and onion; toss to combine. Refrigerate, covered, until chilled, at least 1 hour.

serving provides: 1 Bread, 1 Fruit/Vegetable, 1 Fat.

per serving: 143 Calories, 3 g Total Fat, 0 g Saturated Fat, 1 mg Cholesterol, 352 mg Sodium, 24 g Total Carbohydrate, 5 g Dietary Fiber, 7 g Protein, 120 mg Calcium.

POINTS **per serving:** 2.

make ahead

rush hour

Summer Vegetable Salad with Barley and Pinto Beans

makes 4 servings

Serve this meal in the summer, when corn, tomatoes and basil are at their peak. It is sure to be a hit.

½ cup pearl barley

One 19-ounce can pinto beans, rinsed and drained

2 tomatoes, diced

1 cup cooked corn kernels

4 scallions, thinly sliced

¼ cup chopped basil

3 tablespoons red-wine vinegar

2 teaspoons extra virgin olive oil

½ teaspoon salt

¼ teaspoon freshly ground black pepper

1. Cook the barley according to package directions, either in the microwave or conventionally.

2. In a large bowl, combine the barley, beans, tomatoes, corn, scallions and basil. In a small bowl, whisk the vinegar, oil, salt and pepper. Pour over the bean mixture; toss to coat.

serving provides: 1 Bread, 1 Fruit/Vegetable, 2 Protein/Milks, 1 Fat.

per serving: 246 Calories, 3 g Total Fat, 0 g Saturated Fat, 0 mg Cholesterol, 584 mg Sodium, 48 g Total Carbohydrate, 10 g Dietary Fiber, 10 g Protein, 63 mg Calcium.

POINTS **per serving:** 3.

make ahead

microwave

Good Advice

We all know we need to eat more fiber, yet consuming the recommended 25 to 35 grams of fiber a day isn't always easy—especially if your meals are based on processed foods. Focus on the fact that fiber helps prevent constipation, avert colon and breast cancers, and minimize the complications associated with diabetes. Another bonus: Fiber helps control your appetite (since high-fiber foods tend to be filling), thus boosting your weight-loss efforts.

To up fiber without fuss, always eat a high-fiber breakfast cereal—one that touts at least 5 to 8 grams of fiber per serving—snack on high-fiber fruits, like pears, apples and prunes, or on crispbreads and popcorn; and focus on entrées that are grain-based, such as those using bulgur (cracked wheat), whole-wheat couscous, brown rice and barley.

Salade Niçoise

makes 4 servings

Even without the traditional tuna and anchovy, this Riviera favorite is authentically delicious. If you can find tiny, flavorful Niçoise olives (in gourmet stores), so much the better! The dressing and potatoes can be prepared up to a day in advance, if you like.

5–6 new potatoes (10 ounces), steamed and sliced

1 scallion, minced

1 tablespoon minced parsley

¼ cup Mustard-Vinaigrette Dressing (page 10)

8 cups torn Boston, red leaf or romaine lettuce leaves

1 cup trimmed string beans, steamed and chilled

12 cherry tomatoes, halved

3 eggs, hard-cooked and quartered

10 small pitted black olives

1. In a medium bowl, combine the potatoes, scallion and parsley; drizzle with 2 tablespoons of the dressing and toss to coat. Refrigerate, covered, until chilled, at least 1 hour.

2. In a large salad bowl, arrange the lettuce, potato mixture, beans, tomatoes, eggs and olives in layers in an attractive pattern. Just before serving, drizzle with the remaining 2 tablespoons of the dressing and toss to coat.

serving provides: 1 Bread, 3 Fruit/Vegetables, 1 Protein/Milk.

per serving: 216 Calories, 11 g Total Fat, 2 g Saturated Fat, 159 mg Cholesterol, 156 mg Sodium, 24 g Total Carbohydrate, 5 g Dietary Fiber, 9 g Protein, 127 mg Calcium.

POINTS **per serving:** 4.

make ahead

Spinach-Strawberry Salad

Adding strawberries to a classic spinach salad adds beautiful color, refreshingly sweet flavor—and plenty of vitamin C. With some crusty bread, it's a light meal; but if you like, omit the goat cheese to make a substantial side salad.

1 tablespoon cider vinegar

2 teaspoons corn oil

1 teaspoon Dijon mustard

½ teaspoon honey

Pinch crumbled dried rosemary

Freshly ground black pepper, to taste

One 10-ounce package fresh spinach, cleaned and torn into bite-size pieces

2 cups strawberries, halved

¼ sweet onion, very thinly sliced

⅔ cup crumbled aged goat cheese

1. In a small bowl, whisk the vinegar, oil, mustard, honey, rosemary and pepper.

2. In a large salad bowl, combine the spinach, strawberries and onion; drizzle with the dressing and toss to coat. Sprinkle with the cheese and serve at once.

serving provides: 2 Fruit/Vegetables, 1 Protein/Milk, 1 Fat.

per serving: 137 Calories, 9 g Total Fat, 4 g Saturated Fat, 17 mg Cholesterol, 119 mg Sodium, 10 g Total Carbohydrate, 4 g Dietary Fiber, 8 g Protein, 227 mg Calcium.

POINTS **per serving:** 3.

hint
Refrigerate berries and most other fruits to keep them from spoiling quickly. Since fruits usually taste best at room temperature, remove them from the refrigerator a half hour before eating; wash thoroughly just before serving.

rush hour

Bread and Tomato Salad

makes 4 servings

This Tuscan classic, known as Panzanella, exemplifies the Italian gift of turning the simplest of ingredients into something glorious. Its success depends on two things: fresh-from-the-garden tomatoes and great crusty bread that's at least three days old.

2 tablespoons Vegetable Broth (page 2)

1 tablespoon red–wine vinegar

2 teaspoons extra virgin olive oil

½ teaspoon dried oregano

Pinch salt

Freshly ground black pepper, to taste

4 slices stale crusty peasant bread, cubed (4 ounces)

4 tomatoes, diced

⅔ cup part–skim mozzarella cheese, julienned

½ sweet onion, very thinly sliced

2 tablespoons minced basil

2 tablespoons minced flat–leaf parsley

1. In a small bowl, whisk the broth, vinegar, oil, oregano, salt and pepper.

2. Place the bread in a large salad bowl; sprinkle with enough water to moisten slightly without making soggy. Add the tomatoes, cheese, onion, basil and parsley; drizzle with the dressing and toss to coat. Let stand at least 30 minutes, but no more than 2 hours, to blend flavors.

serving provides: 1 Bread, 1 Fruit/Vegetable, 1 Protein/Milk, 1 Fat.

per serving: 162 Calories, 9 g Total Fat, 4 g Saturated Fat, 22 mg Cholesterol, 266 mg Sodium, 10 g Total Carbohydrate, 2 g Dietary Fiber, 11 g Protein, 267 mg Calcium.

POINTS **per serving:** 4.

make ahead

Pear, Walnut and Feta Salad

makes 4 servings

This elegant main-course salad works well with almost any bitter salad green. If watercress or Belgian endive aren't available, substitute arugula, spinach, chicory, mizuna (Japanese mustard greens)—or any combination.

hint
Add fruit to your salad: Pear and apple chunks are a sweet-tart complement to bitter endive and rich gorgonzola cheese. Mandarin orange sections couple perfectly with artichoke hearts.

1 tablespoon orange juice

1 tablespoon rice or cider vinegar

2 teaspoons corn oil

1 teaspoon Dijon mustard

Freshly ground black pepper, to taste

1 bunch watercress, cleaned

2 Belgian endives, thinly sliced crosswise

2 Anjou or Bartlett pears, cored and cut into 8 wedges each

⅓ cup crumbled feta cheese

¼ cup walnuts, chopped and toasted★

1. In a medium bowl, whisk the orange juice, vinegar, oil, mustard and pepper.

2. Place the watercress and endives in a large bowl. Drizzle with half of the dressing; toss to coat. Add the pears to the medium bowl with the remaining dressing; toss to coat.

3. Divide the greens among 4 plates. Arrange the pear slices over the greens in an attractive pattern, then sprinkle with the cheese and walnuts.

serving provides: 2 Fruit/Vegetables, 1 Protein/Milk, 1 Fat.

per serving: 198 Calories, 12 g Total Fat, 4 g Saturated Fat, 19 mg Cholesterol, 266 mg Sodium, 19 g Total Carbohydrate, 5 g Dietary Fiber, 7 g Protein, 181 mg Calcium.

POINTS per serving: 4.

rush hour

★ To toast the walnuts, place them in a small skillet over medium–low heat; cook, shaking the pan and stirring constantly, until lightly browned, 3–5 minutes.

(See photo insert.)

Tofu "Egg" Salad

makes 4 servings

If you're vegan, prepare this tasty sandwich filling with Tofu Salad Dressing (page 7) or prepared "tofunnaise" from your natural food store; use half the amount of mayonnaise we call for. Stuff the salad in a pita with plenty of lettuce and tomato, or serve it on a bed of lettuce or spinach.

3 tablespoons reduced-calorie mayonnaise or Tofu Salad Dressing (page 5)

2 teaspoons Dijon mustard

½ teaspoon soy sauce

¼ teaspoon turmeric

½ pound Pressed Tofu (page 8), diced

4 celery stalks, diced

1 onion, diced

½ green bell pepper, seeded and diced

1 tablespoon minced parsley

1. In a small bowl, whisk the mayonnaise (or Tofu Salad Dressing), mustard, soy sauce and turmeric.

2. In a medium bowl, combine the tofu, celery, onion, pepper and parsley; stir in the mayonnaise mixture and toss gently to coat. Refrigerate, covered, until the flavors are blended, at least 1 hour.

serving provides: 1 Fruit/Vegetable, 1 Protein/Milk, 1 Fat.

per serving: 120 Calories, 7 g Total Fat, 1 g Saturated Fat, 0 mg Cholesterol, 180 mg Sodium, 8 g Total Carbohydrate, 3 g Dietary Fiber, 7 g Protein, 55 mg Calcium.

POINTS per serving: 2.

make ahead

Falafel Sandwiches

Don't be daunted by the length of the ingredients list—most of these items are common spices and seasonings. This is actually a very easy sandwich to assemble, and it's quite filling.

Falafel

⅓ cup dried chickpeas, picked over, rinsed and drained

⅓ cup packed flat-leaf parsley leaves

½ onion, chopped

2 garlic cloves

½ teaspoon ground coriander

½ teaspoon baking soda

¼ teaspoon ground cumin

¼ teaspoon salt

¼ teaspoon freshly ground black pepper

Pinch cayenne pepper

Sauce

¼ cup fresh lemon juice

¼ cup tahini (sesame paste)

2 tablespoons minced flat-leaf parsley

1 garlic clove

½ teaspoon salt

Sandwich

2 large whole-wheat pitas, halved

1 tomato, sliced

2 cups shredded lettuce

1. Soak the chickpeas using the traditional slow-soak method (see page 5).

2. To prepare the falafel, in a food processor coarsely chop the chickpeas, parsley, onion, garlic, coriander, baking soda, cumin, salt, pepper and cayenne. Let stand 30 minutes; form into 8 patties, about 2 tablespoons each.

3. Spray a medium nonstick skillet with nonstick cooking spray; heat. Add the falafel patties and cook until well browned, 4–5 minutes on each side.

4. To prepare the sauce, in a food processor or blender puree the lemon juice, tahini, parsley, garlic, salt and ¼ cup water.

5. To assemble the sandwiches, line each pita half with tomato slices and lettuce, then add 2 falafel patties; pour in the sauce.

serving provides: 1 Bread, 1 Fruit/Vegetable, 1 Protein/Milk, 1 Fat.

per serving: 307 Calories, 15 g Total Fat, 1 g Saturated Fat, 0 mg Cholesterol, 925 mg Sodium, 34 g Total Carbohydrate, 7 g Dietary Fiber, 13 g Protein, 89 mg Calcium.

POINTS **per serving:** 6.

make ahead

one pot

Grilled Veggie Pitas

makes 4 servings

Grilled vegetables are so hearty and flavorful that they make the perfect sandwich. Grill the veggies ahead of time, but make the sandwiches just before serving.

4 portobello mushrooms

1 medium zucchini, thinly sliced lengthwise

1 red onion, thickly sliced

4 teaspoons olive oil

2 teaspoons balsamic vinegar

1 teaspoon minced thyme

1 garlic clove, crushed

½ teaspoon salt

½ teaspoon freshly ground black pepper

2 large whole-wheat pitas, halved

8 large basil leaves

1. Spray the broiler or grill rack with non-stick cooking spray; set aside. Preheat the broiler or prepare the grill. In a large bowl, toss the mushrooms, zucchini and onion with the oil. Broil or grill the vegetables until just softened, 2–3 minutes on each side.

2. In a small bowl, combine the vinegar, thyme, garlic, salt and pepper.

3. To assemble the sandwiches, line each pita half with the basil leaves and add the vegetables; pour in the vinegar sauce.

serving provides: 1 Bread, 1 Fruit/Vegetable, 1 Fat.

per serving: 149 Calories, 5 g Total Fat, 1 g Saturated Fat, 0 mg Cholesterol, 452 mg Sodium, 21 g Total Carbohydrate, 3 g Dietary Fiber, 7 g Protein, 48 mg Calcium.

POINTS **per serving:** 3.

make ahead

Indian Stuffed Breads

makes 4 servings

This recipe is a simple version of paratha, the Indian flatbread with a flaky texture. Our interpretation is a perfect snack or part of a light lunch—try serving them with Indian Tomato-Lentil Soup (page 18).

½ cup whole-wheat flour

¼ cup all-purpose flour

½ teaspoon salt

1 tablespoon + 1 teaspoon vegetable oil

¼ small cauliflower, cored and grated

½ teaspoon grated peeled gingerroot

Pinch cayenne pepper

1. In a small bowl, combine the flours and ¼ teaspoon of the salt. Add 2 teaspoons of the oil; with your fingers, rub the oil into the flour mixture. Add up to ¼ cup warm water, a little at a time, mixing with your fingers until the mixture forms a dough. Knead the dough in the bowl until soft and pliable, 8–10 minutes. Let stand in a warm place about 30 minutes.

2. In a medium nonstick skillet, heat the remaining 2 teaspoons of oil. Add the cauliflower; cook, stirring as needed, until softened, about 5 minutes. Remove from the heat; stir in the ginger, the remaining ¼ teaspoon of salt and the cayenne.

3. Form the dough into four 4" patties; place the cauliflower mixture in the center of each. Close the dough around the filling and flatten. Dust a work surface with a little flour. Roll each stuffed patty into a 6" round.

4. Spray a small nonstick skillet with nonstick cooking spray; heat. One at a time, cook the dough rounds until golden, about 2 minutes on each side.

serving provides: 1 Bread, 1 Fat.

per serving: 124 Calories, 5 g Total Fat, 1 g Saturated Fat, 0 mg Cholesterol, 299 mg Sodium, 18 g Total Carbohydrate, 3 g Dietary Fiber, 3 g Protein, 12 mg Calcium.

POINTS per serving: 2.

Lentil Burgers

makes 4 servings

These tasty burgers are sure to be a huge hit. Garnish them with your favorite burger toppings. Cook the lentils ahead of time for a fast supper.

½ cup lentils, picked over, rinsed and drained

2 teaspoons olive oil

2 carrots, diced

1 onion, diced

1 teaspoon salt

½ teaspoon minced thyme

½ teaspoon freshly ground black pepper

¼ cup + 2 tablespoons plain dried bread crumbs

4 whole-wheat hamburger buns

1. Cook the lentils according to package directions.

2. In a medium nonstick skillet, heat the oil. Add the carrots and onion; cook, stirring as needed, until golden, 10–12 minutes. Spray the broiler rack with nonstick cooking spray; set aside. Preheat the broiler.

3. Add the lentils, salt, thyme and pepper and 1 cup water to the vegetables; cook, covered, stirring as needed, until the liquid is absorbed, about 20 minutes. Stir in the bread crumbs.

4. Form the mixture into 4 burgers. Broil until golden, 7–8 minutes on each side. Serve on the buns.

serving provides: 3 Breads, 1 Fruit/Vegetable, 2 Protein/Milks, 1 Fat.

per serving: 366 Calories, 7 g Total Fat, 1 g Saturated Fat, 13 mg Cholesterol, 896 mg Sodium, 60 g Total Carbohydrate, 16 g Dietary Fiber, 17 g Protein, 91 mg Calcium.

POINTS **per serving:** 5.

hint
Make your own French "fries" by placing ¼ inch-thick potato slices on a nonstick baking pan and coating them with a light spray of oil. Sprinkle with paprika or salt, and bake, turning once, at 350°F for 35 to 40 minutes. For extra-crisp fries, brush the potato slices with beaten egg whites before baking.

make ahead

Tempeh Sloppy Joes

makes 4 servings

*Kids of all ages will love this vegetarian version of the classic. If you like, make
Cheesy Joes by melting sharp or extra-sharp cheddar on top.*

¼ **pound tempeh, diced**

3 **garlic cloves, minced**

2 **teaspoons olive oil**

1 **green bell pepper, seeded and
chopped**

1 **onion, chopped**

1 **cup Tomato Sauce (page 3)**

1 **teaspoon chili powder**

½ **teaspoon dried oregano**

½ **teaspoon salt**

¼ **teaspoon freshly ground black
pepper**

4 **whole-wheat hamburger buns**

1. In a medium saucepan, combine the tempeh, half of the garlic and 2 cups water; bring to a boil. Reduce the heat and simmer 10 minutes. Drain and pat the tempeh dry.

2. In a large nonstick skillet, heat the oil. Add the pepper, onion and the remaining garlic; cook, stirring as needed, until softened, 8–10 minutes. Stir in the tempeh; cook, breaking up the tempeh with a wooden spoon, 3–4 minutes. Stir in the tomato sauce, chili powder, oregano, salt, pepper and ½ cup water; cook, stirring as needed, until thickened, 8–10 minutes. Serve on the buns.

serving provides: 2 Breads, 1 Fruit/Vegetable, 1 Protein/Milk, 1 Fat.

per serving: 281 Calories, 10 g Total Fat, 1 g Saturated Fat, 13 mg Cholesterol, 554 mg Sodium, 39 g Total Carbohydrate, 8 g Dietary Fiber, 13 g Protein, 79 mg Calcium.

POINTS **per serving:** 5.

hint

Always opt for hard rolls, pitas or whole-grain breads. Avoid croissants, focaccia or any "flaky" breads, which may pack extra fat and calories.

make ahead

Vegetable Cheese Melt

makes 4 servings

This loaf sandwich is crunchy, cheesy, garlicky and filled with vegetables.
Try it for lunch on Saturday with a cup of soup.

4 cups chopped broccoli florets,
   steamed

1 cup shredded part-skim mozzarella
   cheese

¼ cup grated Parmesan cheese

3 tablespoons chopped fresh basil, or
   1 tablespoon dried

1 tablespoon minced fresh thyme, or
   1 teaspoon dried

3 garlic cloves, minced

¼ teaspoon freshly ground black
   pepper

¼ teaspoon salt

One 8-ounce loaf French bread

Preheat the oven to 375°F. In a large bowl, combine the broccoli, cheeses, basil, thyme, garlic, pepper and salt. Split the bread lengthwise almost all the way through; spread open. Fill it with the broccoli mixture, then wrap in foil. Bake until the cheese is melted, 20–25 minutes. Cut the loaf crosswise into 4 portions.

serving provides: 2 Breads, 1 Fruit/Vegetable, 2 Protein/Milks.

per serving: 299 Calories, 8 g Total Fat, 4 g Saturated Fat, 20 mg Cholesterol, 756 mg Sodium, 39 g Total Carbohydrate, 6 g Dietary Fiber, 19 g Protein, 376 mg Calcium.

POINTS **per serving:** 5.

Italian Vegetable Sandwiches

makes 4 servings

Each country in Europe has its own version of this loaf sandwich; these flavors are particularly Italian. It's truly worth seeking out freshly made mozzarella—the kind in your supermarket's dairy aisle is fine for some recipes, but not this one.

hint

Make a grilled cheese sandwich by grating 1½ tablespoons of reduced-fat cheese on the bread, instead of using sliced American cheese.

One 8-ounce loaf whole-wheat or semolina Italian bread

1 bunch arugula, cleaned

2 red bell peppers, roasted★

¼ cup chopped basil

2 tomatoes, sliced

1 red onion, thinly sliced

¼ pound fresh mozzarella cheese, thinly sliced

1 tablespoon +1 teaspoon balsamic vinegar

¼ teaspoon freshly ground black pepper

Split the bread lengthwise almost all the way through; spread open. Line the bottom half with the arugula; top with the roasted peppers, basil leaves, tomatoes, onion and mozzarella. Drizzle with the vinegar and sprinkle with the black pepper. Replace the top half of the bread to enclose. Cut the loaf crosswise into 4 portions.

serving provides: 2 Breads, 2 Fruit/Vegetables, 1 Protein/Milk.

per serving: 238 Calories, 7 g Total Fat, 4 g Saturated Fat, 22 mg Cholesterol, 121 mg Sodium, 34 g Total Carbohydrate, 6 g Dietary Fiber, 12 g Protein, 193 mg Calcium.
POINTS per serving: 4.

rush hour

★To roast bell pepper, preheat broiler. Line baking sheet with foil; place pepper on baking sheet. Broil 4–6" from heat, turning frequently with tongs, until skin is lightly charred on all sides, about 10 minutes. Transfer to paper bag; fold bag closed and let steam 10 minutes. Peel, seed and devein pepper over sink to drain juices.

Veggie Tortilla Roll-ups

makes 4 servings

These fun sandwiches are so easy, and they're a big hit in lunch boxes.
Use your favorite sliced cheese.

Four 6" flour tortillas

¼ cup Tofu Salad Dressing (page 5)

¼ cup chopped basil

½ red onion, thinly sliced

2 tomatoes, thinly sliced

Four ¾–ounce slices cheese

2 cups shredded lettuce

½ teaspoon salt

¼ teaspoon freshly ground black pepper

Warm the tortillas until soft, according to package directions. Spread with the Tofu Salad Dressing; sprinkle with the basil and onion. Layer with the tomatoes and cheese; sprinkle with the lettuce, salt and pepper. Carefully roll up the tortillas; wrap in foil. Refrigerate at least 15 minutes; then cut in half.

serving provides: 1 Bread, 1 Fruit/Vegetable, 1 Protein/Milk.

per serving: 232 Calories, 11 g Total Fat, 5 g Saturated Fat, 19 mg Cholesterol, 876 mg Sodium, 25 g Total Carbohydrate, 2 g Dietary Fiber, 10 g Protein, 180 mg Calcium.

POINTS **per serving:** 5.

(See photo insert.)

make ahead

rush hour

Tofu Burgers

makes 4 servings

Flavored with garlic and tomato sauce, these moist burgers have the great taste of pizza burgers. Melt mozzarella cheese on top for a real treat.

hint

Experiment with virtual burgers: Heat up packaged vegetable or soy burgers in a nonstick pan or the microwave. Serve on crusty rolls topped with ketchup and sautéed onions.

make ahead

2 teaspoons olive oil

1 onion, grated

¼ pound firm reduced-fat tofu, grated

½ medium zucchini, grated

2 garlic cloves, minced

¼ cup Tomato Sauce (page 3)

½ teaspoon salt

¼ teaspoon freshly ground black pepper

¼ cup + 2 tablespoons plain dried bread crumbs

2 tablespoons sunflower seeds

4 whole-wheat hamburger buns

1. Preheat the oven to 400°F. Spray a baking sheet with nonstick cooking spray. In a large nonstick skillet, heat the oil. Add the onion; cook, stirring as needed, until softened, 2–3 minutes. Add the tofu, zucchini and garlic; cook, stirring as needed, until the zucchini is softened, 4–5 minutes. Stir in the Tomato Sauce, salt and pepper; cook, stirring, until thickened, 3–4 minutes. Stir in the bread crumbs and sunflower seeds. Cool to room temperature.

2. Form the mixture into 4 burgers; place on the baking sheet. Bake until browned and firm, 10–12 minutes on each side. Serve on the buns.

serving provides: 3 Breads, 1 Protein/Milk, 1 Fat.

per serving: 292 Calories, 11 g Total Fat, 1 g Saturated Fat, 13 mg Cholesterol, 603 mg Sodium, 40 g Total Carbohydrate, 5 g Dietary Fiber, 11 g Protein, 89 mg Calcium.

POINTS **per serving:** 6.

Super Stacked Salad Sandwiches

makes 4 servings

This combination of salad makings between two pieces of whole-grain bread is particularly tasty. Be sure to use a sturdy bread—sometimes slices of whole-grain breads can be crumbly.

8 slices whole-grain bread

½ medium avocado, peeled and mashed

1 cup cleaned arugula

One 16-ounce jar sliced beets, drained

2 tomatoes, sliced

1 red onion, thinly sliced

1 teaspoon balsamic vinegar

½ teaspoon salt

¼ teaspoon freshly ground black pepper

Four ¾-ounce slices Muenster cheese

Spread 4 slices of the bread with the avocado. On each, layer the arugula, beets, tomatoes and onion. Drizzle with the vinegar, and sprinkle with salt and pepper. Cover with a slice of cheese and a remaining slice of bread. Press down gently and slice diagonally.

serving provides: 2 Breads, 1 Fruit/Vegetable, 1 Protein/Milk, 1 Fat.

per serving: 310 Calories, 12 g Total Fat, 5 g Saturated Fat, 19 mg Cholesterol, 657 mg Sodium, 46 g Total Carbohydrate, 12 g Dietary Fiber, 16 g Protein, 384 mg Calcium.

POINTS **per serving:** 5.

hint

Don't overstuff your sandwiches: A sandwich should have just 2 or 3 slices of filling. If you're craving more filling, stuff away with lettuce, tomatoes, red onion, cucumbers, sprouts and other healthful additions.

rush hour

(See photo insert.)

chapter seven

PIZZA & PASTA

Pizza with "Meat"balls and Mushrooms

makes 4 servings

This is a great version of pizza parlor–style pizza. Vary the flavors of the "meat"balls by using your favorite herbs, or make them spicier with a bit more cayenne pepper.

hint

When it comes to kids, appearance counts: Veggie burgers and pizza as well as tofu hot dogs are kid-friendly; a brick of tofu floating in broth isn't.

2 teaspoons olive oil

½ onion, grated

⅓ cup grated firm reduced-fat tofu

¼ medium zucchini, grated

2 garlic cloves, minced

½ cup + 2 tablespoons Tomato Sauce (page 3)

½ teaspoon freshly ground black pepper

¼ teaspoon salt

¼ cup plain dried bread crumbs

1 tablespoon chopped flat-leaf parsley

1 tablespoon chopped basil

1 teaspoon chopped sage

Pinch cayenne pepper

1 teaspoon cornmeal

½ pound prepared pizza dough

⅓ cup shredded Monterey Jack cheese

2 cups sliced mushrooms

1 teaspoon dried oregano

1. To prepare the meatballs, in a large non-stick skillet, heat the oil. Add the onion; cook, stirring as needed, until softened, 2–3 minutes. Add the tofu, zucchini and garlic; cook, stirring as needed, until the zucchini is softened, 4–5 minutes. Add 2 tablespoons of the Tomato Sauce, ¼ teaspoon of the pepper and the salt; cook, stirring, until the liquid is evaporated, 3–4 minutes. Stir in the bread crumbs, parsley, basil, sage and cayenne. Cool to room temperature; divide into 16 balls.

2. Preheat the oven to 450° F. Sprinkle a heavy baking sheet or pizza pan with the cornmeal.

3. To assemble the pizza, sprinkle a work surface with a little flour; place the dough in the center and roll to coat with the flour. With your fingers, gently stretch the dough to a 5–6" round; roll out to a rough 12" round. Transfer to the baking sheet and pinch the edges to form a rim. Spread with the remaining ½ cup of Tomato Sauce and sprinkle with the cheese; scatter on the meatballs and mushrooms, then sprinkle with the oregano and the remaining ¼ teaspoon of pepper. Bake until the crust is crisp, about 20 minutes.

serving provides: 2 Breads, 1 Fruit/Vegetable, 1 Protein/Milk, 1 Fat.

per serving: 259 Calories, 8 g Total Fat, 2 g Saturated Fat, 10 mg Cholesterol, 464 mg Sodium, 39 g Total Carbohydrate, 2 g Dietary Fiber, 11 g Protein, 124 mg Calcium.

POINTS per serving: 5.

Pizza with Peppers and Ricotta

makes 4 servings

This tomatoless pizza is a pepper lover's dream. Serve it with a salad for a satisfying meal.

1 teaspoon cornmeal

2 teaspoons olive oil

3 red or green bell peppers, seeded and sliced

1 onion, sliced

2 garlic cloves, thinly sliced

¼ teaspoon salt

¼ teaspoon freshly ground black pepper

½ pound prepared pizza dough

1 cup part-skim ricotta cheese

¼ cup chopped basil

1. Preheat the oven to 450° F. Sprinkle a heavy baking sheet or pizza pan with the cornmeal. In a large nonstick skillet, heat the oil. Add the bell peppers, onion and garlic; cook, stirring as needed, until softened, 10–12 minutes. Stir in the salt and black pepper.

2. Sprinkle a work surface with a little flour; place the dough in the center and roll to coat with flour. With your fingers, gently stretch the dough to a 5–6" round; roll out to a rough 12" round. Transfer to the baking sheet and pinch the edges to form a rim. Spoon on the ricotta in small dots; scatter on the sautéed vegetables. Bake until the crust is crisp, about 20 minutes. Sprinkle with the basil.

serving provides: 2 Breads, 1 Fruit/Vegetable, 1 Protein/Milk, 1 Fat.

per serving: 292 Calories, 8 g Total Fat, 4 g Saturated Fat, 19 mg Cholesterol, 395 mg Sodium, 42 g Total Carbohydrate, 4 g Dietary Fiber, 15 g Protein, 199 mg Calcium.

POINTS per serving: 6.

hint
For a speedy lunch, cover a toasted English muffin or mini pita with tomato sauce, shredded part-skim mozzarella cheese and veggies. Heat until the cheese melts.

Caramelized Onion and Tomato Calzone

makes 4 servings

The onions in this stuffed pizza provide a sweet and sophisticated contrast to the tomatoes. The calzones can be made up to 3 days ahead of time; refrigerate them in an airtight container.

2 teaspoons olive oil

8 onions, thinly sliced

Pinch sugar

¼ teaspoon salt

1 tablespoon chopped basil

¼ teaspoon freshly ground black pepper

½ pound prepared pizza dough

3 plum tomatoes, diced

¾ cup shredded part-skim mozzarella cheese

2 tablespoons grated Parmesan cheese

1. In a large nonstick skillet, heat the oil. Add the onions, sugar and ¼ cup water; cook, stirring as needed, until just beginning to color, about 12 minutes. Add the salt and another ¼ cup water; cook, stirring as needed, until the onions are sweet and deep brown, about 30 minutes. Cool; stir in the basil and pepper.

2. Preheat the oven to 450° F. Spray a heavy baking sheet with nonstick cooking spray. Sprinkle a work surface with a little flour; place the dough in the center and roll to coat with the flour. Knead the dough briefly; divide the dough into fourths and roll each into a 6" round. Place 2 rounds on the baking sheet. Divide the onion mixture, tomatoes, and the cheeses between the rounds; cover with the remaining 2 rounds, pinching the edges to seal. Brush the tops with water. Bake until golden, 15–18 minutes; cool slightly before serving.

serving provides: 2 Breads, 1 Fruit/Vegetable, 1 Protein/Milk, 1 Fat.

per serving: 384 Calories, 11 g Total Fat, 5 g Saturated Fat, 27 mg Cholesterol, 571 mg Sodium, 52 g Total Carbohydrate, 5 g Dietary Fiber, 20 g Protein, 378 mg Calcium.
POINTS **per serving:** 8.

make ahead

(See photo insert.)

Spinach and Ricotta Calzone

makes 4 servings

This is a lightened version of the pizzeria classic. Calzones are so easy to make; experiment with your favorite fillings.

2 teaspoons olive oil

1 onion, chopped

One 10-ounce package frozen chopped spinach, thawed and squeezed dry

2 garlic cloves, minced

1 cup part-skim ricotta cheese

½ cup shredded part-skim mozzarella cheese

½ pound prepared pizza dough

1. Preheat the oven to 450° F. Spray a heavy baking sheet with nonstick cooking spray. In a large nonstick skillet, heat the oil. Add the onion; cook, stirring as needed, until softened, about 5 minutes. Stir in the spinach and garlic; cook, stirring as needed, until the spinach is wilted, 4–5 minutes. Let cool slightly and transfer to a medium bowl; stir in both cheeses.

2. Sprinkle a work surface with a little flour; place the dough in the center and roll to coat with flour. Knead the dough briefly; divide the dough into fourths and roll each into a 6" round. Place 2 rounds on the baking sheet. Divide the spinach mixture between the rounds; cover with the remaining 2 rounds, pinching the edges to seal. Brush the tops with water. Bake until golden, 15–18 minutes; cool slightly before serving.

serving provides: 2 Breads, 1 Fruit/Vegetable, 1 Protein/Milk, 1 Fat.

per serving: 293 Calories, 10 g Total Fat, 4 g Saturated Fat, 24 mg Cholesterol, 458 mg Sodium, 35 g Total Carbohydrate, 2 g Dietary Fiber, 17 g Protein, 316 mg Calcium.

POINTS **per serving:** 6.

hint
Although many supermarkets sell prepared pizza dough in the refrigerator case, your local pizzeria or bakery might sell it as well. Ask if they have whole-wheat dough for extra flavor.

Fusilli with Swiss Chard

makes 4 servings

If you're not familiar with Swiss chard, this recipe is an excellent introduction. This vegetable is actually a type of beet that's grown for its broad, deep green leaf rather than for its root. Its flavor is milder than other cooking greens—it's similar to spinach. Reserve the stalks and use as you would celery in another recipe.

1½ cups fusilli

2 teaspoons olive oil

1 onion, chopped

1 bunch Swiss chard, cleaned and chopped

3 garlic cloves, minced

¼ teaspoon salt

¼ teaspoon freshly ground black pepper

1 tomato, diced

1 tablespoon + 1 teaspoon grated Parmesan cheese

1. Cook the fusilli according to package directions. Drain, reserving ¾ cup cooking liquid, and keep warm.

2. In a large nonstick skillet, heat the oil. Add the onion; cook, stirring as needed, until softened, about 5 minutes. Add the chard, garlic, salt and pepper; cook, stirring as needed, until the chard is wilted, about 3 minutes. Stir in the tomato; cook, stirring as needed, until the tomato is softened, 2–3 minutes. Stir in the fusilli and cooking liquid; cook, stirring, 2 minutes. Serve, sprinkled with the cheese.

serving provides: 2 Breads, 2 Fruit/Vegetables, 1 Fat.

per serving: 325 Calories, 4 g Total Fat, 1 g Saturated Fat, 1 mg Cholesterol, 210 mg Sodium, 60 g Total Carbohydrate, 6 g Dietary Fiber, 13 g Protein, 141 mg Calcium.

POINTS **per serving:** 6.

rush hour

Noodles with Spicy Peanut Sauce

makes 4 servings

This dish is similar to the noodles with sesame sauce that are so popular in Chinese restaurants. Make a large batch for a gathering and watch the smiles.

6 ounces linguine

2 tablespoons distilled white vinegar

2 tablespoons smooth natural peanut butter

2 teaspoons grated peeled gingerroot

1 teaspoon vegetable oil

1 garlic clove, crushed

½ teaspoon soy sauce

½ teaspoon Asian sesame oil

¼ teaspoon crushed red pepper flakes

1 cucumber, cut into thin strips

1 red bell pepper, seeded and thinly sliced

4 scallions, thinly sliced

1. Cook the linguine according to package directions. Drain and set aside.

2. Meanwhile, in a large bowl, whisk the vinegar, peanut butter, ginger, vegetable oil, garlic, soy sauce, sesame oil, pepper flakes and 1 tablespoon water. Add the linguine; toss to coat. Add the cucumber and bell pepper; toss again. Sprinkle with the scallions.

serving provides: 2 Breads, 1 Fruit/Vegetable, 1 Fat.

per serving: 247 Calories, 6 g Total Fat, 1 g Saturated Fat, 0 mg Cholesterol, 101 mg Sodium, 41 g Total Carbohydrate, 3 g Dietary Fiber, 9 g Protein, 31 mg Calcium.

POINTS per serving: 5.

hint
Wrap wonton skins around ground chicken or vegetables; then steam. Or wrap fruit and vegetable fillings with rice paper, a Southeast Asian pastry wrapper made from rice flour, water and salt.

make ahead

one pot

rush hour

Good Advice

Not only are beans a great source of soluble fiber (linked to lowering LDL, or "bad," cholesterol) and protein, they are also digested more slowly than other high-fiber foods. The result? You stay full longer and blood sugar levels fluctuate less, so you're less likely to feel hungry. Canned beans are convenient (they can be high in sodium, so rinse them before using), but many people prefer the firmer texture of cooked dried beans (they need to be soaked to rehydrate before cooking them, although dried peas and lentils don't).

Pasta with Chickpeas

makes 4 servings

The combination of chickpeas and pasta is a tradition in Sicily. It is a great meatless pasta that is rich in protein.

1½ cups medium pasta shells

2 teaspoons olive oil

2 onions, coarsely chopped

1 cup drained rinsed canned chickpeas

1 cup crushed tomatoes (no salt added)

2 tablespoons chopped flat-leaf parsley

3 garlic cloves, minced

¼ teaspoon crushed red pepper flakes

¼ teaspoon salt

1. Cook the pasta shells according to package directions. Drain, reserving ½ cup of the pasta cooking liquid, and keep warm.

2. In a large nonstick skillet, heat the oil. Add the onions; cook, stirring as needed, until softened, about 5 minutes. Stir in the chickpeas, tomatoes, parsley, garlic, pepper flakes and salt. Reduce the heat and simmer, stirring as needed, until the tomatoes are softened, about 10 minutes. Stir in the pasta and cooking liquid; cook, stirring, 2 minutes.

serving provides: 2 Breads, 1 Fruit/Vegetable, 1 Protein/Milk, 1 Fat.

per serving: 259 Calories, 4 g Total Fat, 0 g Saturated Fat, 0 mg Cholesterol, 228 mg Sodium, 46 g Total Carbohydrate, 6 g Dietary Fiber, 10 g Protein, 61 mg Calcium.

POINTS **per serving:** 4.

rush hour

Penne with Zucchini and Goat Cheese

makes 4 servings

Goat cheese melts into a rich, creamy sauce. And mint adds a refreshing flavor, although chervil, tarragon or thyme also would be tasty.

1½ cups penne

1 tablespoon olive oil

2 medium zucchini, thinly sliced

½ teaspoon salt

3 ounces goat cheese

2 teaspoons chopped mint

¼ teaspoon freshly ground black pepper

1. Cook the penne according to package directions. Drain, reserving ½ cup of the pasta cooking liquid, and keep warm.

2. In a large nonstick skillet, heat the oil. Add the zucchini and salt; cook, stirring as needed, until very soft, about 10 minutes. Stir in the penne and cooking liquid; cook, stirring as needed, until the liquid is slightly reduced. Then reduce the heat and stir in the goat cheese; simmer, stirring and breaking up with the spoon, until just melted, 1–2 minutes. Sprinkle with the mint and pepper; serve at once.

serving provides: 2 Breads, 1 Fruit/Vegetable, 1 Protein/Milk, 1 Fat.

per serving: 241 Calories, 9 g Total Fat, 4 g Saturated Fat, 10 mg Cholesterol, 373 mg Sodium, 32 g Total Carbohydrate, 1 g Dietary Fiber, 9 g Protein, 45 mg Calcium.

POINTS **per serving:** 5.

rush hour

Penne with Green Beans and Herbs

makes 4 servings

To save time and cooking pots, cook the beans with the pasta.

1½ cups penne

1 pound green beans, cut into 1½–2" lengths

4 teaspoons olive oil

2 garlic cloves, minced

¼ cup chopped flat-leaf parsley

¼ cup chopped basil

½ teaspoon minced thyme

½ teaspoon salt

¼ teaspoon freshly ground black pepper

¼ cup grated Parmesan cheese

1. In a large pot of boiling water, cook the penne 7 minutes; add the beans and cook until the penne is tender, 5–7 minutes longer. Drain, reserving ¼ cup of the pasta cooking liquid, and keep warm.

2. In a large nonstick skillet, heat the oil. Add the garlic; cook, stirring, about 1 minute. Stir in the penne and cooking liquid; cook, stirring as needed, until the liquid is slightly reduced. Remove from the heat; stir in the parsley, basil, thyme, salt and pepper. Sprinkle with the cheese; toss to combine.

serving provides: 2 Breads, 1 Fruit/Vegetable, 1 Fat.

per serving: 253 Calories, 7 g Total Fat, 2 g Saturated Fat, 4 mg Cholesterol, 393 mg Sodium, 39 g Total Carbohydrate, 5 g Dietary Fiber, 10 g Protein, 141 mg Calcium.

POINTS **per serving:** 5.

hint
The starches in the pasta cooking water help to bind the herbs to the pasta, so you don't need to add oil to the dish.

rush hour

Rigatoni with "Meat" Sauce

makes 4 servings

Textured Vegetable Protein, or TVP, is available in some supermarkets and most natural-foods stores. It is made from soybeans and gives this sauce its "meaty" texture.

hint
Try prebrowned
Textured
Vegetable Protein
crumbles (a look-
alike meat
substitute now
widely available in
supermarkets), in
lasagna (layer
TVP as you would
ground beef) and
chili (try a TVP/
bean combo).

2⅔ cups rigatoni

2 teaspoons olive oil

1 green bell pepper, seeded and chopped

1 onion, chopped

½ cup granular TVP

2 garlic cloves, minced

2 cups Tomato Sauce (page 3)

1 teaspoon minced thyme

1 teaspoon chopped oregano

1 bay leaf

¼ teaspoon salt

¼ teaspoon freshly ground black pepper

Pinch crushed red pepper flakes

2 tablespoons chopped basil

1. Cook the rigatoni according to package directions. Drain, reserving ½ cup of the pasta cooking liquid, and keep warm.

2. In a large nonstick skillet, heat the oil. Add the bell pepper and onion; cook, stirring as needed, until softened, 7–8 minutes. Add the TVP and garlic; cook until the TVP is golden, about 3 minutes. Stir in the Tomato Sauce, thyme, oregano, bay leaf, salt, black pepper, pepper flakes and ½ cup water. Reduce the heat and simmer, stirring as needed, until the sauce is thickened and the flavors are blended, about 15 minutes; discard the bay leaf. Stir in the rigatoni and cooking liquid; cook, stirring as needed, until the liquid is slightly reduced, about 3 minutes. Sprinkle with the basil.

serving provides: 2 Breads, 1 Fruit/Vegetable, 1 Fat.

per serving: 287 Calories, 5 g Total Fat, 1 g Saturated Fat, 0 mg Cholesterol, 441 mg Sodium, 47 g Total Carbohydrate, 6 g Dietary Fiber, 15 g Protein, 92 mg Calcium.

POINTS **per serving:** 5.

make ahead

(See photo insert.)

Creamy Spinach and Pepper Lasagna

makes 4 servings

If you can find shredded four-cheese blend (a combination of mozzarella, provolone, Parmesan and Romano), use that instead of the mozzarella in this recipe.

3 cups low-fat (1%) milk

⅓ cup all-purpose flour

2 cups shredded part-skim mozzarella cheese

¼ teaspoon freshly ground black pepper

One 10-ounce package frozen chopped spinach, thawed and squeezed dry

1 cup fat-free ricotta cheese

1 tablespoon olive oil

2 red bell peppers, seeded and sliced

1 onion, sliced

2 garlic cloves, chopped

1 cup pre-browned granular TVP

1 teaspoon fennel seeds, crushed

¼ teaspoon crushed red pepper flakes

8 no-boil lasagna noodles

1. In a large saucepan, heat 2½ cups milk over medium heat until steaming. In a small bowl, whisk the remaining ½ cup of the milk with the flour. Whisk into the hot milk; cook, stirring constantly, until the sauce comes to a simmer and thickens. Continue to cook, stirring, 1 minute. Remove from the heat; whisk in 1½ cups of the shredded cheese and the black pepper.

(See photo insert.)

2. In a medium bowl, stir together spinach and ricotta. Set aside.

3. In a large nonstick skillet, heat the oil. Add the bell peppers, onion and garlic; cook, stirring as needed, until softened, about 5 minutes. Stir in the TVP, fennel seeds, pepper flakes and 2 tablespoons water; cook until heated through, about 3 minutes.

4. Preheat the oven to 400°F. Spray a 9" square baking dish with nonstick cooking spray. With a spatula, spread one-fourth cup of the cheese sauce in the bottom of the dish. Line the bottom with two noodles. Spread with half of the spinach mixture, then another one-fourth cup of the sauce. Add another layer of noodles, then top with all of the sautéed vegetables and another one-fourth cup sauce. Add another layer or noodles and the remaining spinach mixture. Finish with the remaining noodles and sauce. Sprinkle with remaining ½ cup of the shredded cheese.

5. Spray a large piece of foil with nonstick cooking spray, and use it to tightly cover the dish. Bake about 30 minutes; uncover and bake until lightly browned and bubbling, about 10 minutes longer. Let stand 10 minutes before serving.

serving provides: 3 Breads, 1 Fruit/Vegetable, 5 Protein/Milks, 1 Fat.

per serving: 546 Calories, 15 g Total Fat, 7 g Saturated Fat, 44 mg Cholesterol, 519 mg Sodium, 60 g Total Carbohydrate, 5 g Dietary Fiber, 44 g Protein, 975 mg Calcium.

***POINTS* per serving:** 11.

hint
Combine ricotta cheese with mashed, firm tofu to add more protein to your lasagna—it's a great way to sneak more soy into your diet.

make ahead

Fusilli with Roasted Vegetables

makes 4 servings

Roasted vegetables have a rich and hearty flavor; roast them ahead of time for an almost instant supper. This pasta is a delectable treat.

2 red bell peppers, seeded and cut into ½" strips

4 plum tomatoes, cut into thin wedges

2 red onions, slivered

1 medium zucchini, halved lengthwise and sliced

3 garlic cloves, quartered

1 teaspoon minced thyme

¾ teaspoon freshly ground black pepper

1 tablespoon + 1 teaspoon olive oil

1½ cups fusilli

¼ cup finely shredded basil

2 tablespoons grated Parmesan cheese

1. Preheat the oven to 400°F. In a large roasting pan, combine the bell peppers, tomatoes, onions, zucchini, garlic, thyme and ½ teaspoon of the black pepper. Drizzle with the olive oil; toss to coat. Roast, tossing the vegetables once or twice, until the peppers are softened, about 40 minutes.

2. Cook the fusilli according to package directions. Drain, reserving ½ cup of the cooking liquid. Add to the vegetables with the cooking liquid, basil, cheese and the remaining ¼ teaspoon of black pepper; toss to combine.

serving provides: 2 Breads, 2 Fruit/Vegetables, 1 Fat.

per serving: 309 Calories, 7 g Total Fat, 1 g Saturated Fat, 2 mg Cholesterol, 63 mg Sodium, 53 g Total Carbohydrate, 5 g Dietary Fiber, 10 g Protein, 83 mg Calcium.

POINTS per serving: 6.

make ahead

Fettuccine with Creamy Spinach Sauce

makes 4 servings

If you love creamy pasta sauces, remember this recipe—pureed ricotta cheese is a superb alternative to fat-laden heavy cream. To get the smoothest possible texture, be sure to puree it in a blender.

6 ounces fettuccine

2 teaspoons olive oil

½ onion, chopped

1 garlic clove, minced

2 cups chopped cleaned spinach

1 cup canned crushed tomatoes (no salt added)

¼ teaspoon salt

½ cup part-skim ricotta cheese, pureed

¼ teaspoon freshly ground black pepper

Pinch grated nutmeg

1. Cook the fettuccine according to package directions. Drain, reserving ½ cup of the cooking liquid, and keep warm.

2. In a large nonstick skillet, heat the oil. Add the onion; cook, stirring as needed, until softened, about 5 minutes. Add the garlic; cook, stirring, about 1 minute. Stir in the spinach, tomatoes and salt; cook, stirring, until the spinach is wilted, 4–5 minutes. Add the fettuccine, ¼ cup of the cooking liquid and the ricotta; cook, tossing, until just heated through; add more cooking liquid as necessary to make the sauce creamy. Sprinkle with the pepper and nutmeg.

serving provides: 2 Breads, 1 Fruit/Vegetable, 1 Fat.

per serving: 246 Calories, 6 g Total Fat, 2 g Saturated Fat, 9 mg Cholesterol, 217 mg Sodium, 39 g Total Carbohydrate, 3 g Dietary Fiber, 11 g Protein, 140 mg Calcium.

***POINTS* per serving:** 5.

hint
Watch out for faux whole-wheat bread. If it's made from wheat flour, any bread is wheat bread. What's more, some manufacturers add molasses or brown food coloring to make their products appear more wholesome. If the bread feels "squishy" or you can roll it up into a ball, it's as refined as white. Look for "whole-wheat flour" on the ingredients list to make sure you're getting the real thing.

(See photo insert.)

Macaroni and Cheese

makes 4 servings

This is super-cheesy, simple, rich and oh-so-good. Extra-sharp cheddar gives you the most flavor with a smaller amount of cheese. Adding it in batches and stirring it continuously ensures a smooth, creamy sauce. You'll never use a packaged mix again!

1½ cups elbow macaroni

1 cup low-fat (1%) milk

½ onion, grated

2 tablespoons all-purpose flour

2 garlic cloves, crushed

½ teaspoon dry mustard

½ teaspoon salt

¼ teaspoon freshly ground black pepper

Pinch grated nutmeg

1 cup extra-sharp cheddar cheese

1 tomato, diced

1 tablespoon chopped basil

1. Preheat the oven to 350° F. Cook the macaroni according to package directions. Drain and keep warm.

2. In a large saucepan, bring the milk, onion, flour, garlic, mustard, salt, pepper and nutmeg to a boil. Cook, stirring constantly, until thickened, 3–4 minutes. Stir in the cheese in batches until it's melted and the sauce is smooth; stir in the macaroni, tomato and basil.

3. Transfer the mixture to a shallow 1-quart casserole. Bake until golden, 35–40 minutes; cool slightly before serving.

serving provides: 2 Breads, 2 Protein/Milks.

per serving: 313 Calories, 11 g Total Fat, 6 g Saturated Fat, 32 mg Cholesterol, 503 mg Sodium, 39 g Total Carbohydrate, 2 g Dietary Fiber, 15 g Protein, 295 mg Calcium.

POINTS per serving: 7.

make ahead

Spaghetti with Tomatoes, Garlic and Capers

makes 4 servings

Make this dish in the summer, when tomatoes are at their peak, on a night when you need to get dinner on the table in about 20 minutes.

6 ounces spaghetti

4 teaspoons olive oil

1 onion, diced

2 tomatoes, diced

2 tablespoons drained rinsed capers

4 garlic cloves, sliced

¼ cup chopped flat-leaf parsley

½ teaspoon freshly ground black pepper

1. Cook the spaghetti according to package directions. Drain, reserving ¼ cup of the cooking liquid, and keep warm.

2. In a large nonstick skillet, heat the oil. Add the onion; cook, stirring as needed, until softened, about 5 minutes. Stir in the tomatoes, capers and garlic; cook, stirring, until the tomatoes are softened, 3–4 minutes. Add the spaghetti and cooking liquid; simmer until the liquid is slightly reduced, 1–2 minutes. Sprinkle with the parsley and pepper.

serving provides: 2 Breads, 1 Fruit/Vegetable, 1 Fat.

per serving: 228 Calories, 5 g Total Fat, 1 g Saturated Fat, 0 mg Cholesterol, 170 mg Sodium, 38 g Total Carbohydrate, 2 g Dietary Fiber, 7 g Protein, 29 mg Calcium.

POINTS **per serving:** 5.

hint
If you don't have spaghetti on hand, try this dish with any long pasta except capellini—the delicate strands will overcook when you add them to the tomato mixture.

rush hour

chapter eight

GRAIN
& BEAN
SIDE DISHES

Quinoa Tabbouleh

makes 4 servings

This is a traditional tabbouleh salad, made with quinoa instead of bulgur (cracked wheat). Quinoa has a mild flavor, similar to couscous, and its texture is similar to, but lighter than, rice. It's a real nutritional powerhouse—it's a good source of protein, iron and other nutrients. Before you cook the quinoa, rinse it thoroughly to remove the bitter coating.

⅔ **cup quinoa**

2 tablespoons fresh lemon juice

4 teaspoons olive oil

½ **teaspoon salt**

¼ **teaspoon freshly ground black pepper**

2 tomatoes, diced

1 medium cucumber, diced

½ **cup chopped flat-leaf parsley**

4 scallions, thinly sliced

¼ **cup chopped mint**

1. Cook the quinoa according to package directions, either conventionally or in a microwave.

2. In a large bowl, combine the lemon juice, oil, salt and pepper. Add the quinoa, tomatoes, cucumber, parsley, scallions and mint; toss to combine. Let stand until the flavors are blended, 1–4 hours; add more lemon juice if necessary before serving.

serving provides: 1 Bread, 1 Fruit/Vegetable, 1 Fat.

per serving: 168 Calories, 6 g Total Fat, 1 g Saturated Fat, 0 mg Cholesterol, 310 mg Sodium, 25 g Total Carbohydrate, 3 g Dietary Fiber, 5 g Protein, 44 mg Calcium.

POINTS per serving: 3.

make ahead

microwave

Kasha with Apples

makes 4 servings

Kasha is roasted buckwheat groats, a grain with a nutty, toasted flavor. In this dish, it is perfectly complemented by the sweet-tart taste of apple.

1 egg

1 cup kasha

2 teaspoons vegetable oil

1 Granny Smith apple, diced

2 celery stalks, diced

1 onion, diced

1 cup apple juice

¼ teaspoon salt

¼ teaspoon freshly ground black pepper

¼ cup walnuts, chopped and toasted*

1. In a medium bowl, lightly beat the egg; stir in the kasha. Transfer to a small skillet and cook, stirring to separate the grains, until dry, 4–5 minutes.

2. In a medium saucepan, heat the oil. Add the apple, celery and onion; cook, stirring as needed, until the apple is softened, 8–10 minutes. Add the kasha; cook, stirring to coat, about 1 minute. Stir in apple juice, salt, pepper and ¾ cup water; bring to a boil. Reduce the heat and simmer, covered, until the kasha is tender, about 15 minutes. Fluff with a fork and transfer to a serving bowl; sprinkle with the walnuts.

serving provides: 2 Breads, 1 Fruit/Vegetable, 1 Fat.

per serving: 293 Calories, 9 g Total Fat, 1 g Saturated Fat, 53 mg Cholesterol, 186 mg Sodium, 48 g Total Carbohydrate, 2 g Dietary Fiber, 9 g Protein, 40 mg Calcium.

POINTS per serving: 6.

hint Never store fruit in plastic bags (a mold-friendly environment). To ripen fruit faster, place in a sealed paper bag at room temperature for a day or two. The bag traps the gas naturally emitted by ripening fruit, causing it to soften faster.

---

* To toast the walnuts, place them in a small skillet over medium-low heat; cook, shaking the pan and stirring constantly, until lightly browned, 3–5 minutes.

Orzo with Zucchini

makes 4 servings

Although orzo means "barley" in Italian, this is actually a rice-shaped pasta—you'll find it in the pasta aisle of your supermarket.

2 teaspoons olive oil

½ onion, chopped

1 medium zucchini, grated

½ cup orzo

1 garlic clove, minced

¼ teaspoon salt

2 tablespoons grated Parmesan cheese

In a medium saucepan, heat the oil. Add the onion; cook, stirring as needed, until softened, about 5 minutes. Add the zucchini; cook, stirring as needed, until softened, 4–5 minutes. Stir in the orzo and garlic; cook, stirring, until the orzo is just golden, 2–3 minutes. Add 1½ cups water and the salt; bring to a boil. Reduce the heat and simmer, uncovered, until the orzo is tender, about 11 minutes. Serve, sprinkled with the cheese.

serving provides: 2 Breads, 1 Fat.

per serving: 148 Calories, 3 g Total Fat, 1 g Saturated Fat, 2 mg Cholesterol, 195 mg Sodium, 24 g Total Carbohydrate, 1 g Dietary Fiber, 5 g Protein, 48 mg Calcium.

POINTS **per serving:** 3.

one pot

Orange Millet Pilaf

makes 4 servings

Millet is a light, versatile grain—cooking it in orange juice gives it a refreshing and subtle fruity flavor.

2 oranges

¾ cup millet

¼ teaspoon salt

2 teaspoons vegetable oil

1 garlic clove, minced

2 tablespoons chopped flat-leaf parsley

1. Grate the zest from one of the oranges; juice them both. Add water to make 1¼ cups liquid.

2. In a medium saucepan, toast the millet, stirring as needed, until golden and fragrant, 6–8 minutes. Add the orange juice and salt; bring to a boil. Reduce the heat and simmer, covered, until the millet has popped and the liquid is absorbed, 25–30 minutes.

3. In a small nonstick skillet, heat the oil. Add the garlic; cook, stirring, about 1 minute. Stir in the orange zest; cook 10 seconds. Add the garlic mixture and parsley to the millet; fluff with a fork.

serving provides: 2 Breads, 1 Fruit/Vegetable, 1 Fat.

per serving: 197 Calories, 4 g Total Fat, 1 g Saturated Fat, 0 mg Cholesterol, 149 mg Sodium, 36 g Total Carbohydrate, 8 g Dietary Fiber, 5 g Protein, 44 mg Calcium.
POINTS **per serving:** 3.

hint
When cooking rice and other grains according to package directions, omit the butter (the end product will taste the same). Boost flavor by cooking in broth—or even fruit juice—instead of water.

Barley Pilaf with Fruits and Nuts

makes 4 servings

This sweet and nutty mixture is a wonderful combination of flavors and textures. Two kinds of dried fruit and a bit of cinnamon keep things sweet and lively.

2 teaspoons vegetable oil

1 onion, diced

½ cup pearl barley

1 garlic clove, minced

½ teaspoon ground cumin

6 dried apricot halves, chopped

2 tablespoons golden raisins

¼ teaspoon salt

Pinch cinnamon

2 tablespoons slivered almonds, toasted★

In a medium saucepan, heat the oil. Add the onion; cook, stirring as needed, until softened, about 5 minutes. Add the barley, garlic and cumin; cook, stirring, about 1 minute. Stir in the apricots, raisins, salt, cinnamon and 1¼ cups water; bring to a boil. Reduce the heat and simmer until the barley is tender, 45–50 minutes. Add the almonds; toss to combine.

serving provides: 1 Bread, 1 Fruit/Vegetable, 1 Fat.

per serving: 167 Calories, 4 g Total Fat, 0 g Saturated Fat, 0 mg Cholesterol, 151 mg Sodium, 30 g Total Carbohydrate, 5 g Dietary Fiber, 4 g Protein, 33 mg Calcium.

POINTS **per serving:** 3.

make ahead

one pot

★ To toast the almonds, place them in a small skillet over medium-low heat; cook, shaking the pan and stirring constantly, until lightly browned, about 2 minutes.

Good Advice

If you're looking for an alternative to rice, consider one of these "exotic" grains, commonly found in natural food stores, organic markets or mail-order sources.

Amaranth (AM-ah-ranth): A staple of the diet of the Incas and Aztecs, amaranth adds nutty flavor to casseroles. It naturally contains a higher-quality protein (in the form of amino acids) than do most grains, and it is rich in calcium, vitamins A and E, and fiber.

to prepare: Cook 1 cup rinsed amaranth in 1½ cups water or broth for 35 minutes (the grain must be toasted or boiled to make it digestible). Enjoy it in the morning with sliced fruit, or stir into puddings or casseroles. Or combine amaranth with another grain, like wheat flour (¼ amaranth, ¾ wheat) when baking.

Kamut (Kah-MOOT): A member of the wheat family, kamut kernels are rice-like with a buttery-rich taste. It's an excellent source of protein, magnesium, potassium, folate, iron and the B vitamins.

to prepare: Soak whole kamut berries in water overnight; then cook like rice. Serve as a side dish with a sprinkling of Parmesan cheese or stir in some dried fruit.

Quinoa (KEEN-wah): An excellent protein source, quinoa has a more delicate, understated flavor than other grains have. When cooked, the tiny, bead-like granules become fluffy and light. Nutritionally, it's a powerhouse, as quinoa contains all the essential amino acids, plus magnesium and iron.

to prepare: Rinse 1 cup quinoa thoroughly, then sauté in 1 teaspoon olive oil for 1–2 minutes. Add 2 cups of liquid, then simmer or steam for 10–15 minutes. Serve as is or mix, with chopped vegetables for a refreshing cold salad.

Triticale (triht-ih-KAY-lee): A cross between rye and wheat, triticale is a good source of protein, vitamins B and E, copper, iron, magnesium, selenium and zinc. When cooked, these whole berries have a chewy, satisfying texture and can supply pilafs or casseroles with flavor, as well as a nutritional boost.

to prepare: Soak 1 cup triticale in a pan of water overnight. Rinse, then cook in 2½ cups liquid for 40 minutes.

Moroccan Couscous Salad

The flavors and ingredients in this salad are traditional of Moroccan cooking, but the dish itself—a salad—is not.

¾ cup couscous

2 tablespoons chopped flat-leaf parsley

2 tablespoons chopped cilantro

2 tablespoons fresh lemon juice

2 teaspoons olive oil

½ teaspoon paprika

½ teaspoon freshly ground black pepper

¼ teaspoon ground cumin

¼ teaspoon salt

1 carrot, finely diced

½ red bell pepper, seeded and diced

½ cup cooked corn kernels

2 tablespoons chopped red onion

1. Cook the couscous according to package directions.

2. In a large bowl, combine the parsley, cilantro, lemon juice, oil, paprika, black pepper, cumin and salt. Add the couscous, carrot, bell pepper, corn and onion; toss to combine.

serving provides: 1 Bread, 1 Fruit/Vegetable, 1 Fat.

per serving: 317 Calories, 3 g Total Fat, 0 g Saturated Fat, 0 mg Cholesterol, 163 mg Sodium, 62 g Total Carbohydrate, 5 g Dietary Fiber, 10 g Protein, 33 mg Calcium.

POINTS per serving: 6.

rush hour

Curried Rice and Lentil Pilaf

makes 4 servings

This tasty dish is full of the fragrances of Indian cooking. It is a great side dish, but it also fits perfectly in the center of the plate.

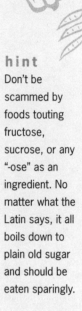

2 teaspoons olive oil

½ onion, chopped

2 garlic cloves, minced

1 teaspoon grated peeled gingerroot

½ teaspoon curry powder

½ teaspoon ground cumin

½ cup lentils, picked over, rinsed and drained

½ cup long-grain white rice

½ teaspoon salt

2 tablespoons chopped cilantro

1 tablespoon fresh lemon juice

1. In a medium saucepan, heat the oil. Add the onion; cook, stirring as needed, until softened, about 5 minutes. Add the garlic, ginger, curry and cumin; cook, stirring, about 1 minute.

2. Add the lentils and 2½ cups water; bring to a boil. Reduce the heat and simmer, covered, about 10 minutes. Stir in the rice and salt; cook, without stirring, until the liquid is absorbed, 15–20 minutes. Let stand 5 minutes, then sprinkle with the cilantro and lemon juice; with a fork, toss to combine.

serving provides: 1 Bread, 1 Protein/Milk, 1 Fat.

per serving: 198 Calories, 3 g Total Fat, 0 g Saturated Fat, 0 mg Cholesterol, 297 mg Sodium, 35 g Total Carbohydrate, 8 g Dietary Fiber, 9 g Protein, 32 mg Calcium.

POINTS per serving: 3.

hint
Don't be scammed by foods touting fructose, sucrose, or any "-ose" as an ingredient. No matter what the Latin says, it all boils down to plain old sugar and should be eaten sparingly.

one pot

Bulgur Pilaf

makes 4 servings

Bulgur is cracked wheat; it's used most familiarly, perhaps, in tabbouleh, but this pilaf is also excellent.

2 teaspoons vegetable oil

1 onion, chopped

1 cup bulgur

1 garlic clove, minced

1 Granny Smith apple, cored and diced

½ teaspoon salt

¼ cup walnuts, chopped and toasted★

¼ cup chopped flat-leaf parsley

1 teaspoon minced thyme

¼ teaspoon freshly ground black pepper

In a medium saucepan, heat the oil. Add the onion; cook, stirring as needed, until softened, about 5 minutes. Add the bulgur and garlic; cook, stirring, about 1 minute. Add the apple, salt and 1¾ cups water; bring to a boil. Reduce the heat and simmer until the bulgur is tender and the water is absorbed, about 15–20 minutes. Add the walnuts, parsley, thyme and pepper; toss to combine.

serving provides: 2 Breads, 1 Fruit/Vegetable, 1 Fat.

per serving: 223 Calories, 7 g Total Fat, 1 g Saturated Fat, 0 mg Cholesterol, 300 mg Sodium, 36 g Total Carbohydrate, 8 g Dietary Fiber, 7 g Protein, 34 mg Calcium.

POINTS **per serving:** 3.

hint

When a recipe calls for nuts, toast them first (the flavor becomes more intense). Simply spread nuts on a baking sheet and place in a 350°F oven; stir occasionally and remove when nuts are golden brown. If you'd rather not heat up the oven, toast them in a nonstick skillet—stirring and shaking the pan often—for about 5 minutes, or heat them in a toaster oven.

one pot

★ To toast the walnuts, place them in a small skillet over medium-low heat; cook, shaking the pan and stirring constantly, until lightly browned, 3–5 minutes.

Polenta with Broccoli Puree

makes 4 servings

The secret to lump-free polenta is to add the polenta to the broth in a thin steady stream while stirring constantly. The easiest way to regulate the speed at which it's added: Put it in your hand and sift it through your fist into the broth.

1 tablespoon + 1 teaspoon olive oil

1 onion, chopped

2 cups Vegetable Broth (page 2)

¼ teaspoon salt

½ cup instant polenta

¼ cup grated Parmesan cheese

2 cups chopped broccoli, steamed

3 garlic cloves, minced

¼ teaspoon minced thyme

2 tablespoons chopped flat-leaf parsley

1. In a medium nonstick saucepan, heat 2 teaspoons of the oil. Add the onion; cook, stirring as needed, until softened, about 5 minutes. Add the broth and salt; bring to a boil. Add the polenta in a thin stream, stirring constantly with a wooden spoon. Reduce the heat and simmer, stirring constantly, until thickened, about 5 minutes. Stir in the cheese.

2. Spray an 8" square baking pan with nonstick cooking spray; spoon the polenta into the pan. Refrigerate, covered, until firm, 1–2 hours.

3. Preheat the oven to 450° F. Spray a baking sheet with nonstick cooking spray. Cut the polenta into 8 triangles; place on the baking sheet. Bake until the edges are golden, about 20 minutes.

4. In a large nonstick skillet, heat the remaining 2 teaspoons of oil. Add the broccoli and garlic; cook, stirring, 5 minutes. Add the thyme and 1 cup water. Reduce the heat and simmer until the water is evaporated and the broccoli is very soft, about 5 minutes. Transfer to a food processor or blender; puree, then pulse in the parsley. Place 2 polenta triangles on each of 4 plates; top with the broccoli puree.

serving provides: 1 Bread, 1 Fruit/Vegetable, 1 Fat.

per serving: 181 Calories, 7 g Total Fat, 2 g Saturated Fat, 4 mg Cholesterol, 303 mg Sodium, 25 g Total Carbohydrate, 4 g Dietary Fiber, 7 g Protein, 120 mg Calcium.

POINTS **per serving:** 3.

hint
Kids are less suspicious of foods they've prepared themselves. Let a little one separate broccoli spears into tiny "trees" or make the salad—even a two-year-old can tear greens and shake the dressing in a small plastic jar.

make ahead

Wild Rice Pancakes

makes 4 servings

These pancakes are chewy yet crunchy; they are delicious with the Cannellini Bean and Escarole Stew (page 81). Be sure that the rice is well-cooked, even a bit overcooked, to keep the rice from absorbing additional liquid and drying out the pancakes.

⅔ cup wild rice

1 cup low-fat (1%) cottage cheese

2 egg whites

2 tablespoons chopped basil

¼ teaspoon salt

¼ teaspoon freshly ground black pepper

1 tablespoon + 1 teaspoon vegetable oil

1. Cook the rice according to package directions, either conventionally or in the microwave.

2. In a medium bowl, combine the rice, cottage cheese, egg whites, basil, salt and pepper. Form into eight 4–5" cakes.

3. In a large nonstick skillet, heat the oil. Add the pancakes, 4 at a time; cook until golden, 3–4 minutes on each side.

serving provides: 1 Bread, 1 Protein/Milk, 1 Fat.

per serving: 186 Calories, 5 g Total Fat, 1 g Saturated Fat, 2 mg Cholesterol, 404 mg Sodium, 22 g Total Carbohydrate, 2 g Dietary Fiber, 13 g Protein, 44 mg Calcium.

POINTS **per serving:** 4.

one pot

microwave

Provençal Lentil Salad

makes 4 servings

This is such a tasty salad. You can serve it right away, but it gets better with time. Make it a day before you plan to serve it to let the flavors develop.

½ cup lentils, picked over, rinsed and drained

½ onion, halved

1 garlic clove, slightly crushed

1 bay leaf

1 red bell pepper, seeded and finely diced

½ red onion, chopped

2 tablespoons chopped flat-leaf parsley

2 teaspoons extra virgin olive oil

2 teaspoons white-wine vinegar

1 teaspoon chopped sage

¼ teaspoon salt

¼ teaspoon freshly ground black pepper

1. In a large pot of boiling water, cook the lentils with the onion quarters, garlic and bay leaf until the lentils are just tender, 20–30 minutes. Drain, discarding the onion, garlic and bay leaf.

2. Transfer the lentils to a medium bowl and toss with the bell pepper, red onion, parsley, oil, vinegar, sage, salt and black pepper. Cool to room temperature before serving.

serving provides: 1 Protein/Milk, 1 Fat.

per serving: 128 Calories, 3 g Total Fat, 0 g Saturated Fat, 0 mg Cholesterol, 152 mg Sodium, 20 g Total Carbohydrate, 9 g Dietary Fiber, 8 g Protein, 28 mg Calcium.

POINTS **per serving:** 1.

hint

Carob claims to be a healthful chocolate alternative, but its fat, sugar and calories are often comparative to the real thing. A smarter idea: Purchase mini-size versions of your favorite candy and practice portion control.

make ahead

Indian-Style Spicy Three-Bean Salad

makes 4 servings

The flavors in this salad are native to the southern part of India. Although Indian cooks would include the seeds and veins of the chile, remember it's a fiery one—seeding and deveining will tame the heat somewhat.

hint
For a fast side dish, select three different types of canned beans; drain and rinse them under cold water. Toss with a chopped bell pepper, tomato, parsley and low-fat vinaigrette.

2 teaspoons vegetable oil

1 teaspoon mustard seeds

2 garlic cloves, sliced

1 serrano chile, sliced (wear gloves to prevent irritation)

⅔ pound green beans, cut into 2" lengths and steamed

1 cup drained rinsed canned black-eyed peas

1 cup drained rinsed canned red kidney beans

¼ cup shredded coconut

2 tablespoons fresh lemon juice

2 teaspoons chopped cilantro

1. In a large nonstick skillet, heat the oil. Add the mustard seeds; cook, covered, until the popping subsides, 1–2 minutes. Add garlic and chile; cook until the garlic is quite fragrant and lightly browned, 2–3 minutes. Remove from the heat.

2. In a medium bowl, combine the green beans, black-eyed peas, kidney beans and co-conut. Add the garlic mixture, lemon juice and cilantro; toss to combine.

serving provides: 1 Fruit/Vegetable, 2 Protein/Milks, 1 Fat.

per serving: 172 Calories, 5 g Total Fat, 2 g Saturated Fat, 0 mg Cholesterol, 287 mg Sodium, 26 g Total Carbohydrate, 9 g Dietary Fiber, 8 g Protein, 76 mg Calcium.

POINTS per serving: 2.

make ahead

rush hour

spicy

Braised Fresh Fava Beans

makes 4 servings

Fresh fava beans are available in the middle of the summer. Choose pods that are not bulging with beans—the bulges mean that the beans are older and tougher. If you cannot find fresh favas, substitute large lima beans and skip the first step.

2 pounds fresh fava bean pods

2 teaspoons olive oil

1 onion, chopped

½ cup dry white wine

2 garlic cloves, minced

½ teaspoon dried thyme

½ teaspoon salt

¼ teaspoon freshly ground black pepper

1 tablespoon fresh lemon juice

1. Remove the beans from the pods; you should have about 2 cups. Bring a large pot of lightly salted water to a boil. Add the beans; cook 30 seconds. Drain, rinsing under cold water; remove the skins.

2. In a large nonstick skillet, heat the oil. Add the onion; cook, stirring as needed, until softened, about 5 minutes. Add the beans, wine, garlic, thyme, salt and pepper; cook, covered, until the beans are tender, about 10 minutes. Stir in the lemon juice.

serving provides: 1 Bread, 1 Fat.

per serving: 161 Calories, 3 g Total Fat, 0 g Saturated Fat, 0 mg Cholesterol, 308 mg Sodium, 24 g Total Carbohydrate, 5 g Dietary Fiber, 6 g Protein, 44 mg Calcium.

POINTS per serving: 2.

hint
Instead of sautéing foods in oil, "sweat" them in broth, tomato juice, wine, even water. You'll save big on calories and fat.

Split Pea–Potato Puree

makes 4 servings

This tasty and brightly colored side dish is an exciting change from ordinary mashed potatoes.

1 tablespoon + 1 teaspoon vegetable oil

3 onions, chopped

2 garlic cloves, minced

1 teaspoon grated peeled gingerroot

½ teaspoon ground cumin

2 large all-purpose potatoes, peeled and cubed

½ cup yellow split peas, picked over, rinsed and drained

¼ teaspoon turmeric

2 tablespoons fresh lemon juice

2 teaspoons chopped cilantro

¼ teaspoon salt

1. In a medium saucepan, heat the oil. Add the onions; cook, stirring as needed, until softened, 7–8 minutes. Add the garlic, ginger and cumin; cook, stirring, about 1 minute.

2. Stir in the potatoes, peas, turmeric and 1½ cups water; bring to a boil. Reduce the heat and simmer, covered, until the peas are tender, 30–35 minutes. Drain any liquid. Transfer to a blender or food processor; puree. Stir in the lemon juice, cilantro and salt.

serving provides: 1 Bread, 1 Protein/Milk, 1 Fat.

per serving: 254 Calories, 5 g Total Fat, 1 g Saturated Fat, 0 mg Cholesterol, 159 mg Sodium, 44 g Total Carbohydrate, 10 g Dietary Fiber, 9 g Protein, 50 mg Calcium.
POINTS per serving: 3.

one pot

Braised Chickpeas

makes 4 servings

The combination of tomato, garlic and mint is traditional of Greek cooking.
This is delicious, so make a large batch—the leftovers are great.

2 teaspoons olive oil

2 onions, chopped

3 garlic cloves, minced

One 19–ounce can chickpeas, rinsed
  and drained

One 14–ounce can diced tomatoes
  (no salt added)

⅓ cup chopped flat-leaf parsley

3 tablespoons chopped mint

½ teaspoon freshly ground black
  pepper

¼ teaspoon salt

2 teaspoons fresh lemon juice

In a large nonstick skillet, heat the oil. Add
the onions; cook, stirring as needed, until softened, about 5 minutes. Add the garlic; cook,
stirring, about 1 minute. Stir in the chickpeas,
tomatoes, parsley, mint, pepper and salt; bring
to a boil. Reduce the heat and simmer, uncovered, until thickened, 10–15 minutes. Stir
in the lemon juice.

serving provides: 1 Fruit/Vegetable, 2 Protein/
Milks, 1 Fat.

per serving: 176 Calories, 4 g Total Fat, 0 g
Saturated Fat, 0 mg Cholesterol, 302 mg Sodium,
27 g Total Carbohydrate, 8 g Dietary Fiber, 8 g
Protein, 91 mg Calcium.

POINTS **per serving:** 2.

hint
Flat-leaf
(sometimes
called Italian)
parsley is more
flavorful but less
attractive than is
its curly leafed
cousin. Use flat-
leaf in cooking,
sprigs of curly for
garnishes.

make ahead

Minted Succotash

makes 4 servings

In this new take on the classic, mint really wakes up the flavors. Fresh corn and lima beans are always the best, but frozen are a fine substitute.

2 teaspoons vegetable oil

1 red bell pepper, seeded and diced

1 onion, diced

½ garlic clove, minced

1 cup fresh or thawed frozen corn kernels

1 cup fresh or thawed frozen lima beans

1 tablespoon chopped mint

¼ teaspoon salt

¼ teaspoon freshly ground black pepper

In a large skillet, heat the oil. Add the bell pepper, onion and garlic; cook, stirring as needed, until softened, about 5 minutes. Add the corn, beans and 1 cup water; simmer, covered, until tender, about 10 minutes. Stir in the mint, salt and black pepper.

serving provides: 1 Bread, 1 Fat.

per serving: 122 Calories, 3 g Total Fat, 0 g Saturated Fat, 0 mg Cholesterol, 174 mg Sodium, 22 g Total Carbohydrate, 6 g Dietary Fiber, 5 g Protein, 23 mg Calcium.

POINTS per serving: 1.

hint

Prepared salads aren't always skinny. Cold pasta in pesto sauce is no slimmer than is the hot variety, and bean and rice salads are often swimming in oil. If the salad is shiny, pass it by.

one pot

rush hour

Boston Baked Soybeans

makes 4 servings

If you think that baked beans without a bit of bacon or pork would taste flat, wait till you try this version. Unlike other beans, soybeans are quite high in fat, so they impart a rich texture, but if you prefer, use navy, great Northern, or any small white bean—you'll cut the total fat by about 14 grams.

2 teaspoons vegetable oil

2 carrots, chopped

2 onions, chopped

1 garlic clove, minced

One 14-ounce can crushed tomatoes (no salt added)

One 15-ounce can soybeans, rinsed and drained

¼ cup molasses or honey

1 tablespoon cider vinegar

½ teaspoon dry mustard

½ teaspoon salt

¼ teaspoon freshly ground black pepper

⅛ teaspoon ground cloves

1. Preheat the oven to 325°F. In a medium nonstick skillet, heat the oil. Add the carrots, onions and garlic; cook, stirring as needed, until softened, 8–10 minutes. Stir in the tomatoes; cook, covered, until slightly thickened, about 5 minutes. Stir the soybeans, molasses, vinegar, mustard, salt, pepper and cloves.

2. Transfer the mixture to a shallow 1½-quart casserole. Bake, covered with foil, about 1 hour; uncover and bake until the beans are very tender and the mixture is quite thick, about 30 minutes longer.

serving provides: 1 Fruit/Vegetable, 2 Protein/Milks, 1 Fat, 50 Bonus Calories.

per serving: 418 Calories, 17 g Total Fat, 2 g Saturated Fat, 0 mg Cholesterol, 327 mg Sodium, 44 g Total Carbohydrate, 11 g Dietary Fiber, 29 g Protein, 259 mg Calcium.

POINTS **per serving:** 8.

make ahead

Good Advice

Studies have shown that diets based on soy foods, such as Textured Vegetable Protein (TVP), tofu and tempeh, might provide protection against heart disease. The protein found in soybeans reduces LDL ("bad") cholesterol, while HDL ("good") cholesterol levels remain unchanged (in people with high cholesterol). Other studies link genistein, a powerful anticarcinogen found in soybeans, with lower cancer rates.

Phytoestrogens, found in soy foods, are hormone-like plant compounds that appear to mimic the effects of estrogen, on a much weaker scale. In menopausal women, who have drastically reduced estrogen levels, these phytoestrogens may help to replace naturally occurring estrogen activity, reducing symptoms of menopause, particularly hot flashes. Soy foods can also help to prevent osteoporosis since soy flour, soy foods and some tofu are good sources of calcium.

White Bean Salad with Lemon and Parsley

makes 4 servings

This refreshing salad is best with great Northern beans.

One 19-ounce can small white beans, rinsed and drained

1 medium cucumber, diced

4 scallions, thinly sliced

¼ cup chopped flat-leaf parsley

2 tablespoons fresh lemon juice

4 teaspoons extra virgin olive oil

1 teaspoon chopped mint

1 garlic clove, crushed

½ teaspoon salt

In a medium bowl, combine the beans, cucumber, scallions, parsley, lemon juice, oil, mint, garlic and salt. Refrigerate, covered, until chilled, at least 1 hour.

serving provides: 2 Protein/Milks, 1 Fat.

per serving: 146 Calories, 5 g Total Fat, 1 g Saturated Fat, 0 mg Cholesterol, 453 mg Sodium, 20 g Total Carbohydrate, 7 g Dietary Fiber, 7 g Protein, 56 mg Calcium.

POINTS **per serving:** 2.

make ahead

Spanish-Style Black Beans

makes 4 servings

In Puerto Rico, these beans are usually served with a steaming pile of rice. The puree of onion, bell pepper and cilantro is called sofrito, *and is a staple in Latin and Caribbean kitchens. Pink beans are traditional, but black beans are also delicious. Experiment to find your favorite.*

2 teaspoons vegetable oil

1 onion, chopped

½ green bell pepper, seeded and chopped

2 tablespoons chopped cilantro

2 garlic cloves, minced

One 19-ounce can black beans, rinsed and drained

¼ teaspoon salt

¼ teaspoon freshly ground black pepper

1. In a large nonstick skillet, heat the oil. Add the onion, bell pepper, cilantro and garlic; cook, stirring as needed, until very soft, 8–10 minutes. Cool, then drain any liquid. Transfer to a blender or food processor; puree.

2. In the skillet, combine the pureed vegetables with the beans, salt, black pepper and ¼ cup water; cook, covered, until the flavors are blended, about 10 minutes. Transfer ¼ cup of the beans to the blender or food processor; puree, then return to the saucepan and heat through.

serving provides: 2 Protein/Milks, 1 Fat.

per serving: 142 Calories, 3 g Total Fat, 0 g Saturated Fat, 0 mg Cholesterol, 307 mg Sodium, 23 g Total Carbohydrate, 7 g Dietary Fiber, 7 g Protein, 52 mg Calcium.

POINTS per serving: 2.

make ahead

one pot

Miso Rice Pilaf

makes 4 servings

If you like Japanese miso soup, you will love this simple pilaf. It has a rich miso flavor and sticky texture.

2 teaspoons vegetable oil

1 onion, chopped

1½ cups chopped cleaned collard greens

⅔ cup medium- or long-grain brown rice

2 teaspoons

1. In a medium saucepan, heat the oil. Add the onion; cook, stirring as needed, until softened, about 5 minutes. Stir in the collards and cook until wilted, about 3 minutes.

2. Add the rice and 1⅓ cups water; bring to a boil. Reduce the heat and simmer, covered, until the rice is tender and the water is absorbed, 35–40 minutes.

3. In a small bowl, dissolve the miso in 2 tablespoons water, stirring as needed. Gently stir into the rice.

serving provides: 1 Bread, 1 Fat.

per serving: 159 Calories, 3 g Total Fat, 0 g Saturated Fat, 0 mg Cholesterol, 112 mg Sodium, 29 g Total Carbohydrate, 2 g Dietary Fiber, 3 g Protein, 22 mg Calcium.

POINTS **per serving:** 3.

hint
Don't have brown rice, or the time it takes to prepare it? Use white rice, but cook in step 2 for only 15–20 minutes.

one pot

chapter nine

EASY VEGETABLE SIDE DISHES

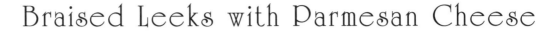

Braised Leeks with Parmesan Cheese

makes 4 servings

Leeks make an elegant and delicious side dish, and they're so easy to prepare. If you think of them primarily as an ingredient in potato-leek soup, next time they're in season (they tend to be expensive) give this simple dish a try.

4 leeks, halved lengthwise and cleaned

1 tablespoon olive oil

¼ teaspoon salt

¼ teaspoon freshly ground black pepper

¼ cup grated Parmesan cheese

Preheat the oven to 350° F. In a 13x9" baking dish, combine the leeks, oil, salt, pepper and ¼ cup water. Bake, covered with foil, until tender, about 25 minutes. Sprinkle with the cheese; bake, uncovered, until the cheese is melted, about 5 minutes longer.

serving provides: 2 Fruit/Vegetables, 1 Fat.

per serving: 129 Calories, 5 g Total Fat, 1 g Saturated Fat, 4 mg Cholesterol, 263 mg Sodium, 18 g Total Carbohydrate, 2 g Dietary Fiber, 4 g Protein, 143 mg Calcium.

POINTS **per serving:** 3.

one pot

Braised Cabbage

makes 4 servings

Sweet-and-sour flavors and cabbage are a match made in heaven. Although we like this with red cabbage, use green if you prefer.

2 teaspoons vegetable oil

1 onion, thinly sliced

½ medium red cabbage, cored and very thinly sliced

½ cup apple juice

1 tablespoon cider vinegar

2 teaspoons sugar

¼ teaspoon salt

1 bay leaf

1 Granny Smith apple, cored and grated

In a large nonstick skillet, heat the oil. Add the onion; cook, stirring as needed, until softened, about 5 minutes. Stir in the cabbage, apple juice, vinegar, sugar, salt and bay leaf; cook, covered, until the cabbage is very tender, about 20 minutes. Discard the bay leaf and stir in the apple; cook, uncovered, about 5 minutes longer.

serving provides: 2 Fruit/Vegetables, 1 Fat.

per serving: 97 Calories, 3 g Total Fat, 0 g Saturated Fat, 0 mg Cholesterol, 156 mg Sodium, 19 g Total Carbohydrate, 3 g Dietary Fiber, 2 g Protein, 52 mg Calcium.

POINTS **per serving:** 2.

hint

If you love cabbage but hate the odor that can linger for days, toss a few large chunks of bread (don't use slices; they can disintegrate) in when you add the cabbage. Discard the bread with the bay leaf.

one pot

Roasted Parsnips

makes 4 servings

Roasting brings out parsnips' natural sugar, making them sweet and succulent.
Combine the parsnips with carrots, celery root and turnips for a real treat.

4 parsnips, peeled and cut into large chunks

2 teaspoons olive oil

¼ teaspoon salt

¼ teaspoon freshly ground black pepper

1 tablespoon chopped flat-leaf parsley

Preheat the oven to 400° F. In a 9"-square baking dish, combine the parsnips, oil, salt and pepper. Roast until tender and browned, about 30 minutes. Sprinkle with the parsley.

serving provides: 2 Breads, 1 Fat.

per serving: 133 Calories, 3 g Total Fat, 0 g Saturated Fat, 0 mg Cholesterol, 160 mg Sodium, 27 g Total Carbohydrate, 7 g Dietary Fiber, 2 g Protein, 54 mg Calcium.

POINTS per serving: 2.

Butternut Squash Puree

makes 4 servings

*This sweet yet garlicky puree will become a family favorite; it's a must
for Thanksgiving.*

2 tablespoons chopped sage

3 garlic cloves, halved

**One 2-pound butternut squash,
halved and seeded**

2 teaspoons reduced-calorie margarine

¼ teaspoon salt

**¼ teaspoon freshly ground black
pepper**

1. Preheat the oven to 400° F. Spray a baking
sheet with nonstick cooking spray. Divide the
sage and garlic between the seed cavities of
the squash. Place, skin-side up, on the baking
sheet. Bake until very tender, about 40 minutes. (To prepare in the microwave, cook the
filled squash in a microwavable dish, covered
tightly.)

2. Scoop the squash, sage and garlic into a
blender or food processor; add the margarine,
salt and pepper and puree.

serving provides: 1 Bread.

per serving: 85 Calories, 2 g Total Fat, 0 g Saturated
Fat, 0 mg Cholesterol, 178 mg Sodium, 19 g Total
Carbohydrate, 3 g Dietary Fiber, 2 g Protein, 78 mg
Calcium.

POINTS **per serving:** 2.

one pot

microwave

Ginger-Roasted Carrots

makes 4 servings

Roasted carrots are naturally sweet; ginger really plays up their depth of flavor.

8 carrots, halved lengthwise

2 tablespoons orange juice

1 tablespoon minced peeled ginger-root

2 teaspoons olive oil

½ teaspoon salt

¼ teaspoon freshly ground black pepper

½ teaspoon grated orange zest

Preheat the oven to 350° F. In a 13x9" baking dish, combine the carrots, orange juice, ginger, oil, salt and pepper. Bake, covered with foil, until tender, 25–30 minutes. Sprinkle with the orange zest.

serving provides: 2 Fruit/Vegetables, 1 Fat.

per serving: 87 Calories, 3 g Total Fat, 0 g Saturated Fat, 0 mg Cholesterol, 341 mg Sodium, 16 g Total Carbohydrate, 4 g Dietary Fiber, 2 g Protein, 41 mg Calcium.
POINTS per serving: 1.

one pot

Broccoli-Potato Puree

makes 4 servings

If you peel the thick stems of the broccoli, you'll find the stalks are quite tender and delicious. Cauliflower can be substituted for the broccoli.

4 small all-purpose potatoes, peeled and cubed

3 garlic cloves

½ teaspoon salt

2 cups chopped broccoli, including stems

1. In a medium saucepan, combine the potatoes, garlic, salt and 1 cup water; bring to a boil. Reduce the heat and simmer, covered, until the potatoes are almost tender, about 10 minutes. Add the broccoli; cook until the broccoli is just tender, about 5 minutes. Drain any liquid.

2. Transfer to food processor; pulse until just smooth. Serve at once.

serving provides: 1 Bread, 1 Fruit/Vegetable.
per serving: 112 Calories, 0 g Total Fat, 0 g Saturated Fat, 0 mg Cholesterol, 316 mg Sodium, 25 g Total Carbohydrate, 4 g Dietary Fiber, 4 g Protein, 48 mg Calcium.
POINTS per serving: 1.

hint
When you're pureeing the potato mixture, be sure to pulse, and watch very carefully. The food processor's speed can make potatoes gluey very quickly.

one pot

rush hour

Good Advice

A vegetarian lifestyle does not limit you when dining in a restaurant. Consider these tips when eating out:

- **Thoroughly review the menu.** Seek out dishes that are touted as vegetarian or heart-healthy.

- **Ask for help.** The waitstaff can help find you a vegetarian selection if one isn't highlighted. A question to ask: Is that prepared with vegetable-based sauce or broth? If necessary, ask if the chef will take a special order.

- **Start with a salad,** preferably one with lots of fresh greens. Order the dressing on the side.

- **Consider the sides.** Order a salad and baked potato with plain yogurt (ask if they have nonfat) on the side. Or create a veggie plate: Ask if the chef will arrange a selection of vegetables on a bed of greens; squirt on lemon juice to add zest.

- **Order berries,** a fresh fruit plate or a cappuccino made with skim milk for dessert.

Roasted Peppers and Eggplant

makes 4 servings

Eggplant lovers will adore this simple side dish.

1 large (1½-pound) eggplant, peeled and cut into 1" slices

¾ teaspoon salt

2 red bell peppers, seeded and thickly sliced

4 teaspoons olive oil

4 garlic cloves, sliced

¼ teaspoon freshly ground black pepper

1. Preheat the oven to 375° F. Place the eggplant on paper towels and sprinkle with ½ teaspoon of the salt. Cover with a plate and press 20 minutes. Rinse and squeeze dry between more paper towels.

2. In a 13x9" baking dish, combine the eggplant, the remaining teaspoon of the salt, the bell peppers, oil, garlic, black pepper, and ¼ cup water. Roast, stirring as needed, until tender, about 45 minutes.

serving provides: 2 Fruit/Vegetables, 1 Fat.

per serving: 94 Calories, 3 g Total Fat, 0 g Saturated Fat, 0 mg Cholesterol, 155 mg Sodium, 17 g Total Carbohydrate, 7 g Dietary Fiber, 3 g Protein, 25 mg Calcium.

POINTS **per serving:** 1.

one pot

Roasted Asparagus

makes 4 servings

Once you've had roasted asparagus, you'll never go back to the watery steamed version again.

2 bunches asparagus, trimmed

1 tablespoon olive oil

½ teaspoon minced thyme

½ teaspoon grated lemon zest

¼ teaspoon salt

⅛ teaspoon fresh ground black pepper

Preheat the oven to 425° F. On a baking sheet, combine the asparagus, oil, thyme, lemon zest, salt and pepper. Roast until tender, tossing once, 10–15 minutes.

serving provides: 1 Fruit/Vegetable, 1 Fat.

per serving: 60 Calories, 4 g Total Fat, 0 g Saturated Fat, 0 mg Cholesterol, 151 mg Sodium, 4 g Total Carbohydrate, 4 g Dietary Fiber, 4 g Protein, 36 mg Calcium.

POINTS per serving: 1.

one pot

rush hour

Broccoli with Chinese Flavors

makes 4 servings

This is a light version of the popular garlic-and-ginger sauce from Chinese restaurants.

1 cup orange juice

2 teaspoons cornstarch

1 tablespoon soy sauce

2 teaspoons grated peeled gingerroot

2 garlic cloves, minced

¼–½ teaspoon crushed red pepper flakes

1 teaspoon Asian sesame oil

4 cups chopped broccoli, steamed

In a small saucepan, mix 2 tablespoons of the orange juice and the cornstarch to form a thin paste. Gradually stir in the remaining orange juice, then stir in the soy sauce, ginger, garlic and pepper flakes; bring to a boil. Reduce the heat and simmer until thickened, 3–4 minutes. Remove from the heat and stir in the oil. Drizzle over the broccoli.

serving provides: 2 Fruit/Vegetables.

per serving: 92 Calories, 2 g Total Fat, 0 g Saturated Fat, 0 mg Cholesterol, 298 mg Sodium, 17 g Total Carbohydrate, 5 g Dietary Fiber, 5 g Protein, 80 mg Calcium.

POINTS **per serving:** 1.

hint
For perfect steamed veggies, don't overcrowd the steamer basket and cook the vegetables only until they are tender crisp (hint: they should be brightly colored and firm).

one pot

rush hour

spicy

Sautéed Watercress

makes 4 servings

Since watercress grows in water, it doesn't have the grit that most greens do. Eliminating the tedious washing—just give it a quick rinse—makes this the fastest vegetable dish ever.

2 teaspoons olive oil
3 garlic cloves, minced
2 bunches watercress, cleaned
¼ teaspoon salt

In a large nonstick skillet, heat the oil. Add the garlic; cook, stirring constantly, until fragrant, about 1 minute. Add the watercress; cook, stirring, until just wilted, 2–3 minutes. Sprinkle with the salt and serve at once.

serving provides: 1 Fruit/Vegetable, 1 Fat.

per serving: 27 Calories, 2 g Total Fat, 0 g Saturated Fat, 0 mg Cholesterol, 160 mg Sodium, 1 g Total Carbohydrate, 0 g Dietary Fiber, 1 g Protein, 44 mg Calcium.

POINTS **per serving:** 1.

hint

Dandelions are beloved as a vegetable, but cursed as a weed: this sharp-flavored green adds bite to salads; it's also delicious sautéed with a little garlic. To avoid the risk of pesticides, purchase dandelion greens rather than picking them yourself.

one pot

rush hour

INDEX

Metric Conversions

If you are converting the recipes in this book to metric measurements, use the following chart as a guide.

Volume		Weight		Length		Oven Temperatures	
¼ teaspoon	1 milliliter	1 ounce	30 grams	1 inch	25 millimeters	250°F	120°C
½ teaspoon	2 milliliters	¼ pound	120 grams	1 inch	2.5 centimeters	275°F	140°C
1 teaspoon	5 milliliters	½ pound	240 grams			300°F	150°C
1 tablespoon	15 milliliters	¾ pound	360 grams			325°F	160°C
2 tablespoons	30 milliliters	1 pound	480 grams			350°F	180°C
3 tablespoons	45 milliliters					375°F	190°C
¼ cup	50 milliliters					400°F	200°C
⅓ cup	75 milliliters					425°F	220°C
½ cup	125 milliliters					450°F	230°C
⅔ cup	150 milliliters					475°F	250°C
¾ cup	175 milliliters					500°F	260°C
1 cup	250 milliliters					525°F	270°C
1 quart	1 liter						

Dry and Liquid Measurement Equivalents

Teaspoons	Tablespoons	Cups	Fluid Ounces
3 teaspoons	1 tablespoon		½ fluid ounce
6 teaspoons	2 tablespoons	⅛ cup	1 fluid ounce
8 teaspoons	2 tablespoons plus 2 teaspoons	⅙ cup	
12 teaspoons	4 tablespoons	¼ cup	2 fluid ounces
15 teaspoons	5 tablespoons	⅓ cup minus 1 teaspoon	
16 teaspoons	5 tablespoons plus 1 teaspoon	⅓ cup	
18 teaspoons	6 tablespoons	⅓ cup plus two teaspoons	3 fluid ounces
24 teaspoons	8 tablespoons	½ cup	4 fluid ounces
30 teaspoons	10 tablespoons	½ cup plus 2 tablespoons	5 fluid ounces
32 teaspoons	10 tablespoons plus 2 teaspoons	⅔ cup	
36 teaspoons	12 tablespoons	¾ cup	6 fluid ounces
42 teaspoons	14 tablespoons	1 cup plus 2 tablespoons	7 fluid ounces
45 teaspoons	15 tablespoons	1 cup minus 1 tablespoon	
48 teaspoons	16 tablespoons	1 cup	8 fluid ounces

Note: Measurement of less than ⅛ teaspoon is considered a dash or a pinch.